T0090873

THE
MANDATE

AN INSPIRATIONAL GUIDE

MYRA A. COOPER

WESTBOW
PRESS®
A DIVISION OF THOMAS NELSON
& ZONDERVAN

WestBow Press books may be ordered through booksellers or by contacting:

WestBow Press
A Division of Thomas Nelson & Zondervan
1663 Liberty Drive
Bloomington, IN 47403
www.westbowpress.com
844-714-3454

Scripture quotations are from the King James Version of the Bible.

ISBN: 978-1-6642-0805-6 (sc)
ISBN: 978-1-6642-0806-3 (e)

Print information available on the last page.

WestBow Press rev. date: 03/09/2021

DEDICATION

This book is dedicated to my wonderful children, Nevin my son and Nakera, my daughter. They have been most supportive in my endeavors to write and the completion of this book. Their support has encouraged me in my plight to make this Inspirational Guide to follow The Mandate, which God sent each of us to earth to complete in bringing others to know Him.

PREFACE

The Mandate is written to help you live a successful Christian life. It is designed to show you how to invest in yourself, to know you are worthy before God, therefore enhancing your walk before both God and man. These are not two different things, as many people separate their walk with God as Spiritual and attend Church regularly doing church activities with church people (walking with God). Then they view their careers apart from their Christianity and at work they display a different self, by getting into the competition of moving forward in their career (walking with man). Hence many do not even say that they have a connection to God (while not at church). This book will show you how to grow in Spirit; how to release your soul to God; how to govern the behaviors of your body wherever you are. You will then become successful within yourself first, then among those around you and in that which you do.

In short, it is written to show you how to live victoriously on the earth, and to bring those whom you love, meet and or work with, to knowing the One True God. This is the Mandate given to each one who would accept the Lord Jesus Christ into their heart as Personal Savior. You are not expected to speak from a Podium or be a Pastor if you have not been called to that Ministry by God. The message in The Mandate shows you how to stay on the right course throughout the remainder of your life. Many churches do a new converts course for new Christians, but seemingly this is not enough, as many new converts turn back and go into the world's way of life again. Also, on the other hand, many people after giving their heart to the Lord just end up sitting on the (bench) pew. This gives the feeling of when a player, in a ball game is confined to sitting on the bench. This is not God's Will, every Christian has been given a Mandate to bring others to Christ, that is, make disciples, but unfortunately, some are not being encouraged to do so. Thus, living their entire lives as babes in Christ, dying and going on to Heaven, never having experienced the maturity and blessing of leading another person to Him.

Jesus came to earth, to redeem man back to God. This is the reason He died for us on the Cross. We will stand before God one day and would there be someone else whom we've led to Christ with us? "And Jesus came and spoke unto them saying, all power is given unto me in Heaven and in earth. Go ye therefore and teach all nations, baptizing them in the name of the Father and of the Son and of the Holy Ghost: Teaching them to observe all things whatsoever I have commanded you: and lo, I am with you always, even unto the end of the world. Amen (Matthew 28:18-20(KJV)." Jesus is our Teacher, we are his disciples. Therefore, a disciple emulates his teacher, Jesus. It is every Christian's duty to follow and complete The Mandate He has set for us.

CONTENTS

KNOWING GOD

———◆◆◆———

Have you ever met God? In most countries the local or common citizens are not allowed access to walk up to the Palace or the Great House, either the House of Parliament, the Government House or the White House, built for the residence of the leader, and just walk in for a visit. As a citizen of your country, if you were to request a meeting with the elected official, or Head of State, which would be either the Prime Minister, The Premier, or the President, would you be granted a favorable response? The Office Aides to the Head of State, may be very polite in seeking from you the reason for your request and they may even carry out some investigation on you, for security purposes, but it is highly unlikely that you would be allowed a direct visit. On the other hand, depending on your status in society, you may not be viewed as someone of very high importance to be making such a request in any event and therefore, you may not be granted clearance to visit. This is the method of world leaders and you may believe that if it is so difficult to meet a world Commander in Chief, how much more difficult it is to meet and talk to God. There is also a belief that all religious roads lead to Jehovah God's Heaven, but this is far from the truth and here's why:

First, He's God of the entire Universe, and He both speaks and listens. He is waiting to listen and speak answers to your questions back to you. He longs for relationship with you because He loves you, and you do not have to be of a certain caliber or race to be welcome in His presence.

Secondly, you will find that when you understand that He indeed loves you, it would be easier to ask Him anything. Even if you do need to meet with a Head of State, with Him nothing is impossible and if you believe, it can happen at the right time. Your love for him will grow even as your knowledge will increase more and more. When you love someone, it is easier to accept them as a friend. You can very easily do the same with God, He wants to be your friend.

Third, God created us with the ability to speak and hear, even as He speaks and hears. We were created in His image. Therefore, He is waiting to have a dialogue with us. But the Bible does say that we were born in sin and created in iniquity (wicked, sinful, evil, criminal). So, because God is Holy, and we are sinners, it is important that we should be on the same page with God so that we can be in right standing to speak to Him and hear His responses.

The first record of God and man having dialogue was in the Garden of Eden, with Adam and Eve, after He created them and placed them in the Garden to Live. He visited with them and had conversation with them, this would be in the cool of the day when He would call out to them talking with them regularly. But eventually they did not follow God's instructions completely and sinned, when they ate the fruit from the tree which God had forbidden them not to touch (Genesis 3:8(KJV). Then they became afraid of God's presence in the garden because of their sin. So, God had to expel them from the Garden of Eden.

Now because God had been trying to reach man since then, He sent His son, Jesus into the world to die for the sins of mankind (which would be you and me), which Jesus did when He was crucified. This means that Jesus then becomes the link between God and man. But before I proceed further, it is necessary that you know that you have a friend (God), who understands you, and wants you to hear and walk close to Him. This cannot happen unless you know God personally. He is indeed waiting to receive you and be your Father God. Now because of what happened with Adam and Eve in the Garden of Eden, this means that after that time, everyone born into the world was born into sin. "For as by one man's disobedience, many were made sinners, so by the obedience of one shall many be made righteous." (Romans 5:19KJV)

The Fourth reason for you to be in a good position to talk to God, you must accept Him through Jesus Christ in your heart, by confessing your sins to Him. Romans 10:9(KJV) states, "That if thou shalt confess with thy mouth the Lord Jesus, and shall believe in thine heart that God had raised Him from the dead, thou shall be saved." But that confession is for verbal speakers. Many are also non-verbal who read and write. They can believe God for Salvation within their heart. John 3:16 says, "For God so loved the world that He gave His only Begotten Son, that whosoever believeth in Him should not perish, but have everlasting life. Those who are verbal may also pray this prayer. Romans 10:9 is for those who wish to hear themselves speak the prayer. If you pray this prayer to God through Jesus Christ and believe it from your heart you will be saved. This is a prayer of repentance which leads you to become a Christian and make ready for Heaven. Let's pray:

Dear Jesus, I know I am a sinner, so I wish to repent.
Please forgive me of my sins and come live in my heart.
Make me a new person and show me how to
Be an example to others.
Thank you for dying to save me from sin. Amen!

If you believe this prayer, you have been born again. To become born again means that you are now saved from sin, your sins have been forgiven and you have received the Holy Spirit, He lives within you now, meaning He knows you. **You have now met God through Jesus!** Your name has been recorded in Heaven, and all the Angels are rejoicing that you are now a Child of God. It means you have been justified (meaning you're vindicated) by God now that you have repented from sin. It is like you have never sinned, and if you should die today, you will go to Heaven. Accepting Jesus into your Heart as Savior changes your destiny forever. **He's the best friend ever!**

WELCOME TO GOD'S FAMILY!

At sixteen years of age, I repented of my sins and gave my heart to God through Jesus Christ. It's been over fifty years now. I was the first one to do so in my family of eleven and it was very hard and not at all easy for me. My family attended the Episcopal Church, but I received Christ and became a born-again Christian in the Baptist Church. That alone was difficult for me, as I pressed to attend church where I first believed and was now being trained by the Word of God. My eyes were opening to the fact that God loved me unconditionally and expected that I live for Him. My mother, whom I love dearly, objected forcefully when it was time for me to go to church and the rest is history.

I prayed for my mother for twenty-eight years before she accepted and received Jesus into her heart. The interesting and important thing for me is that God used me to pray with her, thus introducing her to know Him. This was at a time when she had become very ill and I was visiting with her at the Hospital. She was ready to receive Jesus into her heart and the time was right, Praise the Lord, my mom is living in Heaven today. I came through because The Holy Spirit was with me and I know it could only have been God that brought me through many, many times, just as He lives in you. Since having accepted Jesus into my heart, I have led numerous persons to Christ under His direction. Be encouraged, as you follow the instructions written in this guide, it will give you a clear grasp of Prayer and The Word, you will make it. Hold on to God He will never let go of you as you follow the Mandate, He's set for you as a Christian.

Now that you have met God through Jesus Christ, it's time to grow in strength in your relationship with Him, He is our Father and Friend, and Jesus our elder Brother. Now you have been saved for a purpose, which is to help to lead others to Him. "And we have seen and do testify that the Father sent the son to be the Savior of the world (1 John 4:14(KJV))." Father, God sent Jesus into the world to die for us and redeem us back to Him. God called Abraham His friend because Abraham fully trusted God without question, even though he did not know where he was going, he remained obedient to God. "And the scripture was fulfilled which says, Abraham believed God, and it was imputed unto him for righteousness: and he was called the Friend of God." (James 2:23) When we are obedient and trust God, believing that He is holding us, this Pleases God.

Know that your purpose is unique, and God's Will is that you grow stronger in Him and fulfill it. There are many Christians who may have come to salvation for many years, but they seemingly show very little signs of growing stronger in their walk with God, because they are simply unaware that they should spend time with God and hear Him speak to them. Spending time with God, is done by taking time to meet with Him in your secret place or prayer closet. Most Christians pray each night before going to sleep, thanking God for the day's events and seeking His further protection. This is good, but we should worship Him every chance we get, not just when we turn in for the night, or go to church to fellowship with the other worshippers.

It is important therefore to find a place in your home where you can meet alone with God each day. If you are young and do not share a bedroom with other siblings, you can pray in your bedroom. Here is where you pray, sing from your heart, as well as sing along with worship songs, read The Word and Meditate on it. This is a time when you can Worship Him from your heart. Make sure you have your Worship sessions in enough time so that you do not interrupt your time to prepare for your daily activities. You will find that at first you may not know what to say to God. Your prayers at first may only last two to three minutes, you have just begun so do not be discouraged, God rejoices over you, and in your humbleness and honesty, He will prompt you in your spirit what you ought to pray about, it may even be that you need to pray for your neighborhood and people you know who have not accepted Jesus as yet. But remember, at this time in your life no one can do it for you, except your being open to The Lord, Just Trust Him.

It is good to learn to talk to The Lord about everything. In this way, you will get to know Him even more and you will get a clearer understanding of why you are here on the earth and that is to destroy the works of the devil. Never believe that The Lord is only interested in the great activities that go on in your personal life. He's interested in the well-being of your family members, who your friends are, where you live, healthy eating habits, what you wear, any illnesses you may encounter, financial difficulties and increase of the same, where you worship God and employment concerns, just to name a few. In fact, God is interested in everything that is connected to you. He is a good, good Father and He truly wants you to do life with Him, pressing to live under His direction. You will find that God will hear and answer your prayers, once your prayers are in accordance with His Word. For this reason, the study of God's Word is most important. I have found that for me the best time to meet with God is in the early morning.

For us today, we may not physically hear God walking in the Garden like Adam and Eve, but we know that He speaks within our Spirit when we pray in communication with Him. Our God is a speaking God, who loves to hear and answer prayer. Now as we Pray, Study the Word and Worship the Lord, let's be open to understanding more of how this makes us live upright in this world. Let's Pray:

Dear Lord, as I read this Book give me an understanding heart to comprehend and put into practice what you are saying to me. Show me how to follow your direction in staying on the right course, and help me to always love and trust you with my whole being. Thank You for loving me, in Jesus Name! Amen!

Understanding
God's Word

ecause of the way life's experiences are played out or designed, we can very easily feel that God has forgotten about us. These can come in the form of roadblocks, to getting good job opportunities because of not having been afforded the privilege to go to college, or even send our children to college because of finances. When one is unable to move forward, it seems their life is being held back by the enemy. "But I will sing of Thy Power; yea, I will sing aloud of thy mercy in the morning: for thou hast been my defense and refuge in the day of my trouble (Psalm 59:16(KJV)." This is where Faith (confidence in God) becomes most important because God's Will is that we walk by faith. His Holy Spirit gives us the confidence we need to listen for His voice within our own spirit. His Voice will give the direction that is needed to save us from pain and unnecessary disappointment. Our hardships do not bring Glory to Him when we experience unfortunate circumstances.

Hosea 4:6(KJV) says, "My people are destroyed for lack of knowledge: because thou hast rejected knowledge, I will also reject thee, that thou shall be no priest to me: seeing thou hast forgotten the law of thy God, I will also forget thy children." In other words, we cannot expect to be excused because we did not know something that was important. Therefore, it is crucial that Christians equip themselves by knowing

God's Word as much as possible so that we stay on the right course. To hear the Voice of God will cost much investment of your time. As you will soon discover many of the human voices you are accustomed to, will have to be ignored when you begin to seek more of God's Voice. Our Mandate as Christians is to bring others to know Him, but we can only be effective if we know His Word.

Now as you read the Word of God, there will be certain scriptures, maybe only one or two verses in a scripture passage that will stand out or move within your spirit. These scriptures show that God speaks to us personally through His Word and when certain scripture verses stand out, it is meant for you to take note. You may hear and understand something, that has not registered in the spirit of another person. For instance, **"Blessed are the pure in heart: for they shall see God."** (Matthew 5:8(KJV)** First, you pray about it, asking God for a clear understanding of this Word. Then I am sure He will open His Word in your spirit to understand that your **heart** within is to be kept **pure**. "Create in me a clean heart, O God; and renew a right spirit within me (Psalm 51:10(KJV)." It's not only that we keep our outer lives somewhat clean so that the world may see and believe that we are living decent and clean. If the heart is unclean, we can very easily allow negative and unholy thoughts and acts to fester within the soul. Your heart is the real you!

In most societies in the western world, people are accustomed to go to church every week as it is what they have been taught to do. But it doesn't say that they have committed their heart totally to God. To attend church regularly does not make one a Christian. That one only turns out to be a good Church attendee, rather than a candidate for Heaven. God wants to be your Father and He wants to have a genuine relationship with you and to be the keeper of Body, Soul and Spirit. It is why He sent His Son Jesus, to earth to die on the cross for you and me. His desire for us is that when the time comes for you to leave this world, He wants you to live in Heaven with Him.

When you were a child beginning Kindergarten, your parents or guardian began to instill proper discipline within you. Their teachings, along with other responsible adults which include, grandparents, older siblings, teachers at school and church all contributed. This meant that you were taken to School, Church, Sports and other positive Youth Clubs etc. where you followed instructions as you participated in the activities and interactions with others, which were necessary to prepare you for adulthood. Eventually, you found yourself graduating from high school and later college. Those close to you knew that proper discipline would lead you to be a successful adult, and you would be equipped with the necessary training and maturity to choose a profession and at the right time raise a family of your own.

Now it is most important to understand that in order to grow into a mature Christian, there are some things you would need to do and adopt as life principles to stay on the right course so that you will not compromise your Christian walk. Make prayer, the reading, study and meditating on God's Word a daily habit. This will strengthen you to grow spiritually, as it will draw you closer to God. You will then find that you'll begin to understand what you are reading and be guided by that which the Word is instructing you and the hearing of His Voice within your spirit will become clearer.

I believe we have been given the gift of The Bible, which is designed to give us the answers to every life situation we may encounter, and it is why The Holy Spirit caused it to be written. The Bible is paramount in lifting your spirit up. It is meant to open the eye consciously in the spirit, and the revealing of how every Christian should live. God has indeed designed it to surely help you stay on the right Course. "All scripture is given by inspiration of God, and is profitable for doctrine, for reproof, for correction, for instruction in righteousness. That the man of God may be perfect, thoroughly furnished unto all good works." (2 Timothy 3:16, 17(KJV) This means that the Word of God has been given by Him that we may understand how to live righteously and well prepared how to live in this world. The Word teaches what is right or wrong, and whatever the situations, whether right or wrong, it is designed to put you on the right path.

The Word of God, corrects, instructs and/or rebukes as necessary and it is designed to prepare us to be completely ready for all that God has for you to do in the earth. Even as you now know that God speaks, He will not twist your arm and make you listen to what He wishes you to hear from Him. If He is willing to speak, then you should be fully prepared to listen. Some ways we can hear Him speak to us are:

Through our personal study of His Word. This should be enough as the more one studies, the more understanding is revealed into the spirit. I would suggest that new Christians begin with areas of the Bible that would be easier understood, like the Gospels – Matthew, Mark, Luke, and John; and the Psalms and Proverbs. It may not be advisable to read the Book beginning at Genesis Chapter 1 and ending at Revelation Chapter 22. This can easily become disenchanting, as areas of both the Old and New Testament are more difficult to follow without assistance. Should you wish to go that route, it may be beneficial to speak with your Pastor, Bible Study teacher, or another grounded Christian for help in this area. The best area of the Bible to read first is the Gospel of Saint John. This Book is easiest to understand and comprehend. It would give you a good grasp of the Words Spoken by Jesus.

This means that it is most beneficial to be aligned to a church where the Word of God is taught in truth and there is a Pastor to watch and pray for your spiritual success along with the study of the Word, which is most important. "Not forsaking the assembling of ourselves together, as the manner of some is: but exhorting one another: and so much the more, as ye see the day approaching (Hebrews 10:25(KJV)." You will surely grow with the fellowshipping with other like-minded Christians. It will also help if you are pressing through difficult situations in any area of life, there should be other believers there who can give words of encouragement and prayers. Therefore, one should be prayerful in choosing the right church, trusting God for Guidance.

God gives visions and dreams to his children which are understood to be Supernatural signs. It may be that a hurricane or a violent storm may be coming over an area of land, namely the city where you live. God is saying, pray for that city and/or if you live in the area prepare. It may even be that something wonderful is going to happen and He could be directing and reassuring us to give thanks within our spirit.

Then read loud enough to hear yourself when studying the Word. You will find that you'll remember more of what you read and make it a habit to read every day. Sometimes we try to read the Bible through because someone else is doing it. Then it becomes a task, we hardly remember what we've read as we try to rush through it. But when we take the time to read the chapters slowly, more than once in your own hearing, you'd find just how grounded you are when the right Word would come into you spirit just at the time you need it.

You are encouraged to prayerfully rely on the Holy Spirit Who would speak to you within your spirit, giving you a clear understanding of the Word as you read it. Meditate on what you read as the Word of God helps you make right decisions for daily living in the event a crisis occurs within your life. "And to make all men see what is the fellowship of the mystery, which from the beginning of the world hath been hid in God, who created all things by Jesus Christ:" (Ephesians 3:9(KJV)

You may have young children of your own or you're involved with children, nieces, nephews, Teach Sunday school, or professional School Teacher. In order to teach them by instilling good examples within their spirit, you'd have to be well informed into the Word of God. Study well to have a good grasp of God's Word. "Study to show thyself approved unto God, a workman that do not need to be ashamed, rightly dividing the word of truth." (2 Timothy 2:15(KJV)

Each person is born not knowing God in a personal way, but after one comes to know Jesus Christ through Salvation, The Holy Spirit imparts knowledge as they study and understand the written Word of God. "But the natural man receiveth not the things of the Spirit of God: for they are foolishness unto him: neither can he know them, because they are spiritually discerned (1 Corinthians 2:14(KJV)."

TRUSTING GOD THROUGH HIS WORD

———— ◆ ————

I t is important that we are capable to hear from God, if we are to stay on the right course throughout our Christian life. Therefore, studying His Word is the key in helping us hear His Voice, as it is the foundation we should build upon. Spending time in God's Word, makes it easier to detect error in interpretation when it is spoken in our hearing. One example is, to experience a difficult time whether it is an illness, family, or job situation, most likely the Believer may be told that it is God's Will that they are suffering because God is teaching them a lesson. Such a statement is incorrect, because the Word says, "Surely He hath born our grief and carried our sorrows: yet we did esteem Him stricken, smitten of God, and afflicted. But He was wounded for our transgressions, He was bruised for our iniquities: the chastisement of our peace was upon Him; and with his stripes we are healed (Isaiah 53:4-5(KJV)." God does not deviate from what He has said.

When one travels to an unfamiliar place, The Global Positioning System (GPS) is very useful and important in keeping one on the right course or direction so as not to get lost during transit, because if you mistakenly deviate from the instructions given, you can very easily wander off course. Imagine being on the way to an important meeting, and you turn off onto the wrong road, then you know you will arrive late at your destination. Or travelling very late at night, and mistakenly take the wrong course. Immediately the GPS would begin to assist in getting you on the right course and it does an efficient job.

Even more so, when we make The Word of God our map for living, we soon realize that we're growing spiritually and can depend on His Word for success. Even as the enemy uses untrue tactfulness by placing false imaginations within the spirit, or confuse a situation through others, thus taking one off the right course. Knowing God's Word will keep you focused. When we fail to follow His Voice through His Word, we end up regretting decisions or taking wrong directions. When we do not adhere to the written guidelines given in the Word of God, we cause hardship on ourselves if we are not taught sufficiently in the Word. In other words, ignorance is no excuse, when the Word is open for us to study, understand, and follow. "Thy Word is a lamp unto my feet, and a light unto my path." (Psalm 119:105(KJV)

Knowing the Word of God guides us in making wise decisions, thereby keeping us from ignorant or untoward behavior. The Holy Spirit makes us capable of studying God's Word and understanding His Voice through His Word, but the enemy will seek to mix the Word with subtle imaginations which he craftily plants within the thoughts at first. These thoughts are never the complete truth and usually not how it is written in the Bible. "The simple believeth every word: but the prudent man looketh well to his going." (Proverbs 14:15(KJV) Therefore, one cannot rely alone on what is heard on Christian Television, Social Media, or even some Preachers, make sure what you are hearing can be backed up with what God's unadulterated Word says. Which means, we've got to know His Word.

Remember the serpent was successful in deceiving Eve (Adam's wife). He questioned Eve in such a manner, that she probably felt that she was foolish and thought it was God who had deceived her, "Yea, hath God said, Ye shall not eat of every tree of the garden? And the woman said unto the serpent, we may eat of the fruit of the trees of the garden:

But of the fruit of the tree which is in the midst of the garden, God hath said, Ye shall not eat of it, neither shall ye touch it, lest ye die. And the serpent said unto the woman, Ye shall not surely die: For God doth know that in the day ye eat thereof, then your eyes shall be opened, and ye shall be as gods, knowing good and evil." (Genesis 3: 1-5(KJV) He succeeded in getting Eve to believe that God was being unreasonable with them. The Serpent's statements made Eve feel that God was trying to double-cross or cheat them (Adam and Eve) out of a privilege that should have been theirs. But when all was said and done, Adam and Eve were left with the pain of sin and shame.

How many times does Christians feel cheated, when they don't have sufficiency for life, e.g. finances or Career opportunities. Satan's motive is to malign the Name of God, by making our witness of Jesus appear to be warped or untrue. Satan was successful in leading Eve into the sin of the pride of life, by getting her to believe she could be just like God. "For all that is in the world, the lust of the flesh, the lust of the eyes, and the pride of life, is not of the Father, but is of the world." (1 John 2:16(KJV) These sins began when Adam and Eve sinned by disobedience to God. Every sin that man can commit would fall under one of these three areas, the lust of the flesh, the lust of the eye, and the pride of life.

When we resist the devil, he has to flee. Now how does one resist the devil? You should oppose him in whatever way he presents himself to you, which is through others, usually those you love and respect or within your own spirit. It is usually by flattery and promises, through cunning, deception and threatening either within your own mind or through another. When this happens, firmly resist him by refusing to do what he expects you to comply with, and you will see that he will flee from you. "Be sober, be vigilant; because your adversary the devil, as a roaring lion, walketh about, seeking whom he may devour." (1 Peter 5:8(KJV)

The enemy operates through strategies against God's people. His plan is their total failure and/or demise. But Prayer along with the understanding of God's Word and constant Worship, singing Praises to Him, are keys that would keep us on the right course. This will certainly propel you into living out what you have learnt through the Word and The Holy Spirit through prayer will give you the strength to persevere. "Praying always with all prayer and supplication in the Spirit and watching thereunto with all perseverance and supplication for all saints:" (Ephesians 6:18(KJV).

In the preceding paragraph, we spoke about The Holy Spirit. He is the third Person of the Godhead or the Trinity (God the Father, God the Son, God The Holy Spirit). When we are born-again and become Christians, we are now born of the Spirit. "Jesus answered and said unto him, Verily, verily, I say unto you, except a man be born again, he cannot enter into the Kingdom of God (John 3:5(KJV)." The Holy Spirit is sent by God to be a helper to Believers. He is the Spirit of Truth walking alongside us after Jesus returned to Heaven. When we go against the Word of God, and do what we wish, then we can grieve the Holy Spirit.

Prayer is making our petitions known to God, after which we expect an answer. The enemy seeks to keep us from embracing this Divine Privilege with God. Therefore, when we Pray, we should approach The Father in Jesus' Name, not asking for anything that does not comply with The Word of God, "And in that day ye shall ask me nothing. Verily, verily, I say unto you, whatsoever ye shall ask the Father in My Name, He will give it you. Hitherto have ye asked nothing in My Name: ask, and ye shall receive, that your joy may be full," (John 16:23-24(KJV)

While Jesus was praying one day, one of His disciples asked Him to teach them to pray, just as John taught his disciples. Jesus therefore gave them the outline of prayer. "And He said unto them, when ye pray, say, Our Father which art in Heaven, Hallowed be Thy Name.

Thy Kingdom come. Thy Will be done, as in Heaven, so in earth. Give us day by day our daily bread. And forgive us our sins; for we also forgive everyone that is indebted to us. And lead us not into temptation but deliver us from evil. (Luke 11:2-4(KJV)." The Lord's Prayer is made up of the beginning, the petitions and the conclusions. When I was a girl, this prayer was called, "The Lord's Prayer. It gives Christians a pattern to follow while praying.

This means that when we come before God in prayer, in the first instance it is important to acknowledge and give him thanks for Who He is, the privilege He gives us to come before Him, and what He means to us. "But thou, when thou prayest, enter into thy closet, and when thou hast shut thy door, pray to thy Father which is in secret; and thy Father which seeth in secret, shall reward thee openly (Matthew 6:6(KJV)." Thank Him for His Grace and Mercy toward you. It is good to ask for His forgiveness of your own wrongs and misdeeds and the forgiving of those who have done you wrong. This is before we begin talking to God about blessings and concerns you may have for others.

Petitions are naturally whatever one needs to talk to God about, which may be for salvation, and healing, blessings in the lives of others (which include neighbors, friends, your country and the wider world); your family members, both immediate, extended and yourself; the Ministry where God has planted you; that peace surround your country and all who live there just to name a few petitions. "Ye lust and have not: ye kill and desire to have, and cannot obtain: ye fight and war, **yet ye have not, because ye ask not** (James 4:2(KJV)." We pray because God has promised and ordained that He will act on our behalf when we pray. He wants to do for us those things which we cannot do for ourselves, but we have got to talk to Him about it.

Then the conclusion is to always acknowledge the name of Jesus. We pray for Peace and Joy in the lives of families, colleagues, Churches, our own Personal Ministries, business organizations, our Nation, other Nations and the World. When we are finished praying to Father

God, we should acknowledge the Name of Jesus, who intercedes to the Father on our behalf. Therefore, we should always end by saying, "In the Name of Jesus," Amen!

When we trust God, it means we will watch what we say after we have prayed and it builds our confidence. To talk negatively it hinders our prayers being answered. We will continue to forgive others from the heart and not judge them, God will bless us. Even as we cannot change what has already happened to us and prayer helps us to heal in our spirit so that we don't get bitter with life itself. When we trust God, He will cover us in every circumstance He will look out for our well-being causing that which we need to be dealt with precisely. "Ask and it shall be given you; seek, and ye shall find; knock, and it shall be opened unto you: (Matthew 7:7(KJV)" God knows exactly how to bring peace to us in every situation. Prayer is pertinent in changing our own life so we can be useful in and toward the lives of others.

THE PURPOSE
OF PRAYER

———————◆———————

P rayer is communicating or simply talking with God. Earnest prayer is meant to take you into God's Presence. He waits to hear you and wants you to hear from Him. Our duty is to wait for His Answer after we have prayed. Sometimes His Answer is Yes, No, or Wait which means at the right time all will be well. Even if He says no within our spirit, this is to help us to press in asking what direction to take in a matter. When we know our prayer has been answered our confidence grows stronger in Him, as He paid the price when He died for us. As our risen Lord, He's given us clearance to talk to Father God, through Him intimately as long as we like and whenever we wish.

Earnest prayer is knowing that He is listening, strengthening and encouraging you to walk by faith. "He that dwelleth in the secret place of the Most-High shall abide under the shadow of the Almighty." (Psalm 91:1(KJV) Your secret place is living in and believing God by faith. Because if we do not believe by faith, then we are not pleasing Him, so let us prayerfully stay with God. He will bring our earnest desires to pass. So let's allow him to be the master of our lives! He is just a prayer away and you can talk to Him from wherever you are. There is no need to dress up your prayers with fancy words to be accepted.

There are teachings about various kinds of prayer, but for this guide it is important to know that your prayers are acceptable when you pray in faith believing. God just wants you to believe that He is who he's always said, and that He rewards us when we believe Him. So, pray believing, that you will hear from God. "But without faith it is impossible to please Him: for he that cometh to God must believe that He is, and that He is a rewarder of them that diligently seek Him. (Hebrews 11:6(KJV)

"Enter into His Gates with Thanksgiving, and into His Courts with Praise: be thankful unto Him, and bless His Name (Psalm 100:4(KJV)." Before you begin to talk to The Lord about yourself, your concerns, others, or whatever else is important to you, it may even be world hunger and disaster in your country or neighborhood; first honor Him with your lips and a heart of praise. Tell Him that you love Him, giving Him the Highest Praise – HALLELUJAH! Thank the Holy Spirit for His Presence, guarding, guiding, directing, providing and His protection over you. "If ye shall ask anything in my name, I will do it." (John 14:14(KJV) This means we are praying under God's authority, and we believe that He will do what we are asking. Let us not forget to respectfully express our gratitude for all that He's done and continues to do. Honor Him from your heart with Thanksgiving, Singing and Praises. It brings Him Glory!

Prayer changes things, so when we come before The Lord, we should come not just asking, but seeking with sincerity, believing by faith that God has heard us. We would not know how to pray and/or ask in the right way, but His Spirit, through His Grace, helps our weaknesses, and literally intercedes for us with groanings which we cannot humanly explain. (Romans 8:26, 27, 28(KJV) Then we wait for His answer, which when it comes, we understand that Prayer truly does change things. "If ye then, being evil, know how to give good gifts to your children, how much more shall your Father which is in heaven give good things to them that ask Him?" (Matthew 7:11(KJV) God's desire is for us to live clean and victorious lives on the earth but the only way it can happen is if we take the time, as many times a day as we need, to meet with Him in prayer. But before we even begin to pray, we should examine ourselves to make sure we are clean, and our body and inner selves (spirit, soul, and body) are fit to come before Him.

Most Believers do not get caught up in Adultery and Fornication, which they may only look on as sin, but they have no problem in engaging in so many other types of sin, even though to them they are small. But God is Holy and wants us to be like Him. So, when we present ourselves to Pray, we should first confess our own wrong behavior before Him. It's not just those deeds which we call big sins like Adultery, fornication, murder, or stealing from others, i.e. gossiping, deceitfulness, petty insults to others, being mean spirited and speaking petty lies, etc. which they may feel are small sins. "If we confess our sins, He is faithful and just to forgive us our sins, and to cleanse us from all unrighteousness. (1 John 1:9(KJV) Even as throughout the day one is praying during the day's activities within one's spirit. This brings you into more intimacy with God, and indeed draws you closer into His presence, which pleases Him.

Most people take the time to be alone intimately with their spouse, in order to bond as one in spirit. Responsibly thinking parents spend quality time with their children, so that they may bond as a family. Many persons even take time out to share and visit with close relatives and friends, to encourage and lift each other up. Church groups put on social events for their parishioners, and Professional companies may even take a little time out during the year for a social event for employees, all for the purpose of bonding as a team.

Every aspect of your life should include prayer, so make prayer a lifestyle. Spend time talking to God and wait to hear Him speak, into your spirit. Even if you do not pray aloud, you will find yourself praying within your spirit, in a meeting, at school, talking to family members, driving in your vehicle, taking a stroll in your yard, etc. "Rejoice evermore. Pray without ceasing. In every- thing give thanks:

for this is the will of God in Christ Jesus concerning you. Quench not the Spirit." (1 Thessalonians 5:16-19(KJV) Make every effort to bond with God, your Father. Even more so, believers should develop close intimacy with God every day and meet Him in that special quiet place. It is where you tell God not only your troubles, but to receive answers to your questions and get direction for life. "But thou, when thou prayest, enter into thy closet, and when thou hast shut thy door, pray to thy Father which is in secret, and thy Father which seeth in secret shall reward thee openly." (Matthew 6:6(KJV)

Find that secret place to meet God each day. God walked in the Garden where Adam and Eve lived at the cool of the day, (Genesis 3:8(KJV) but they allowed the Adversary to lead them off the right course God had set for them and lost fellowship with Him. God's walking with Adam and Eve signified relationship and fellowship with them. God sent His Son, Jesus who came and gave us the privilege through salvation in Jesus. We can have intimacy with God through Prayer.

We cannot spurn our relationship with Him, but we must take advantage of this gift from God, even as The Holy Spirit lives in us. Through prayer, He will teach us how to conduct our lives in times when there seems to be trouble looming, or in hard situations when nothing seems to be working out right, or when we do not feel like praying. It is then when He will tell you what to say at just the right moment, or not say anything at all to anyone, but to allow your spirit to pray inwardly. Prayer brings maturity within us and we understand things that otherwise we would never know, because they are revealed to us by The Holy Spirit.

Getting Results
through Prayer

Pray according to The Word, especially when you need an on-time answer from The Lord. "For the Word is quick, and powerful, and sharper than any two-edged sword, piercing even to the dividing asunder of soul and spirit, and of the joints and marrow, and is a discerner of the thoughts and intents of the heart." (Hebrews 4:12(KJV) An example of praying for a quick answer is when you fear you may be in danger. Take for instance, you may have to travel into an unsafe area late at nighttime, and you need God's protection. "Yea, though I walk through the valley of the shadow of death, I will fear no evil: for Thou art with me; Thy rod and Thy staff they comfort me." (Psalm 23:4KJV); Also, "He shall call upon me, and I will answer him: I will be with him in trouble; I will deliver him and honor him." (Psalm 91:15(KJV)

Say to God exactly what you mean, and exactly what you are asking to happen in a situation. Examples may be, you wish to see a loved one saved; purchase a home; excel in school examinations; desire healing from an illness for yourself or a loved one etc. Jesus has placed our promises on his account, so through grace by faith we have whatever we desire if it is in accordance with God's Word. "(As it is written, I have made thee a father of many nations,) before him whom he believed, even God, who quickeneth the dead, and calleth those things which be not as though they were." (Romans 4:17(KJV)

Now believe you have received your request. It is done not only in spirit, but you have the tangible results also. When we believe by Faith we receive. Faith is having confidence that God will do what we asked. "Therefore, I say unto you, what things soever you desire, when you pray, believe that you receive them, and ye shall have them." (Mark 11:24(KJV) When we fail to let Faith grow within us, we become unsettled in all our ways, moving around like one without a resting place. Let us believe God, regardless to whatever we see happening before us. If God said it, believe it, this is exactly what Faith is.

One reason for not receiving answer to prayer is when one refuses to forgive an injustice done to them. When we do not forgive, we can easily harbor a root of bitterness within, which can only grow in our own lives, and we find we not only become bitter over the first issue, but every other little thing that happens thereafter. Forgiving others quickly is most important as it brings healing and releases our own spirit into peace. God is unable to answer our prayers if we carry matters of not forgiving others in our heart. "And when we stand praying, forgive, if ye have aught against any: that your father also which is in heaven may forgive your trespasses (Mark 11:25(KJV)." Father God does not tell us to forgive so that he might punish us. He knows what's best for us and continuing without forgiving brings continual anger, whereby our spiritual growth and our health can be attacked.

It is important to understand that even as we forgave the first time we got offended, we very easily find it difficult to completely let it go and the enemy tries to see to it that we do not let it go. Thus, Believers find it difficult to totally forgive, forget and let it go. When someone does or says something terrible about the character of another and they know what they are saying is untrue and other Believers tend to hold on to what has been said, then it becomes quite difficult to, 'just let it go'. "Then came Peter to Him, and said, Lord, how oft shall my brother sin against me, and I forgive him? Till seven times? Jesus saith unto him, I say not unto thee, until seven times: but, until seventy times seven (Matthew 18:21, 22(KJV)." My interpretation, if one has been terribly hurt or wronged, it would indeed be difficult to immediately forget, but when forgiving an awful deed done to them, in prayer as often as necessary, eventual healing would be realized, then one can in fact, truly let it go. Total, forgiveness usually winds up being a process, meaning it is best to forgive every time you think about the injustice or hurt done to you, which may end up being seventy times seven.

Eventually the hurt subsides, and you know in your heart you have truly forgiven. Especially when you don't become hurt or angry when you interact again with those persons for any reason. Forgiving also helps that one who has been hurt not to experience depression. Also pray for those who have done you an injustice and watch God change them to become better soldiers for the Lord. On the other hand, there are consequences for those having deliberately slandered another, doubles down and never ceasing. "Rest in the Lord and wait patiently for Him: fret not thyself because of him who prospereth in his way, because of the man who bringeth wicked devices to pass. Cease from anger and forsake wrath: fret not thyself in any wise to do evil. For evildoers shall be cut off: but those that wait upon the Lord, they shall inherit the earth. (Psalms 37:7-9(KJV)."

Another reason we may not receive answer to prayer, is when we are not humble enough to apologize to another. As Believers we have a duty to apologize when we have done wrong or erred in our treatment toward others. In recent years I have heard some Christians say that apologizing is unnecessary, as it is not clearly stated in the Bible, and Christians are not obligated to say they are sorry for the wrong they have done to another. Apologizing does not mean one is expected to go into a lengthy discussion of what happened. The one needing to apologize should at least say, I'm sorry, or I misspoke. "Depart from evil and do good; seek peace and pursue it (Psalm 34:14(KJV)." Most of us grew up in homes where our parents saw to it that we apologized for either saying or doing something wrong to our siblings or friends. We had to do it with sincerity, or you were made to apologize over and over until you sounded sincere and did not roll your eyes or display a bad attitude or you were really punished with the switch. I also followed this same pattern with my own children, and it worked. They have indeed grown up to be respectful and responsible adults.

Not apologizing for wrongs done to others is not a good example to set for the youth of today. Also not apologizing does not make one free of their wrong-doing before God. "Confess your faults one to another, that ye may be healed. The effectual fervent prayer of a righteous man availeth much. (James 5:16(KJV)" We apologize to others for the wrongs we have done, as it brings peace between friends, families and sets a good example.

Prayer does not have to be lengthy with intense moaning, as some may believe. One does not have to shout at God to get Him to understand the seriousness of the situation so He can act on your behalf. It can be short and simple, to the point, by faith believing that your Father God has heard you. "And this is the confidence that we have in him, that, if we ask anything according to His Will, he hears us: And if we know that he hears us, whatsoever we ask, we know that we have the petitions that we desired of Him." (1 John 5:14, 15(KJV)

We have all mistakenly and unknowingly prayed the wrong way in the past. But we did not understand why we did not receive an answer to what we were requesting from God. Yes, it is true that God sometimes says to wait, but eventually, He causes us to understand why it was not safe for us at a certain time. Unanswered prayer can also be because we did not pray correctly or prayed amiss. God will listen to our prayers and answer them when we pray in accordance with His Word. Humbly Give Him His Word back as much as possible through prayer, as God does not deny His Word.

Here's how to pray including God's Word. God knows what His Word says, you do not have to say the chapter and verse where it is found. "If ye shall ask anything in my name, I will do it. (John 14:14(KJV).":

Father I know prayer changes things, and I thank you for changing my situation at (e.g. work, home, school, or any area of importance) Even as your Word says, I can ask anything in Your Name and You would hear and answer me. Now I thank You for seeing me through this Difficult time, and the peace you are giving to me. Amen!

It could be that we are not praying in faith believing, even if we are asking for the right thing. One can very easily be praying in fear and not by faith. Lack of faith can especially seep in, if a tragic situation has occurred. It may be a serious doctor's diagnosis etc. While we cannot ignore the seriousness of such a terrible circumstance, it is also not correct to disbelieve the Lord when He's already told us, "Fear thou not, I am with thee: be not dismayed; for I am thy God: I will strengthen thee; yea, I will uphold thee with the right hand of my righteousness." (Isaiah 41:10(KJV) Which means, stop worrying!

It can be easy to allow yourself to slump into fear, anger, and fretful uncertainty, even as one may genuinely cry out to God for victory, feeling this is the right thing to do. But with fear present within our spirit, we block our prayers from being answered. The Word of God tells us that fear is sin. "Be careful for nothing, but in everything by prayer and supplication, with thanksgiving, let your requests be made known to God; and the peace of God, which passeth all understanding, shall keep your hearts and minds through Christ Jesus." (Philippians 4:6, 7(KJV) The Word tells us to pray and remain in thanksgiving to God for the answer and when He does, we will know by His Spirit that He has answered.

Fear that is not dealt with, can cripple our outlook on life and be the cause of anxiety attacks. Fear can truly cause medical problems such as serious stomach aches, depression, loss of sleep among other conditions. Therefore, it should be given to God through prayer and the commitment of our lives totally to Him. This will surely be realized when along with prayer, read scriptures that can encourage your spirit. "Trust in The Lord with all thine heart; and lean not on thine own understanding. In all thy ways acknowledge Him, and He shall direct thy paths." (Proverbs 3:5,6(KJV). When you become anxious because of fear, praying will bring peace to the heart, and you will feel that His Presence brings peace to you.

My experiences have been that as one grows stronger into their Christian walk, in living and being a witness for The Lord, the enemy works feverishly to bring fear and doubt into the spirit to cause us to fail. He knows we will not turn away from serving God, so he just does not want us to be successful in that which we do for the Kingdom of God. Colossians 3:15(KJV) explains, that to conquer fear, honor the Lord with everything within you, praise Him often, looking out for the well-being of others with songs of praise. The Holy Spirit will help you. In my own experience, I have had to press in this way when facing hard situations, it brings peace to the spirit.

Our prayers may not be answered when we ask God for something with wrong motives. God knows what our intentions are because He is all knowing. Persons may wish to show off certain accomplishments to show themselves as being in a higher social and financial standing than others. Sometimes they may not have a need for what they are requesting from God. Christians should not seek to get ahead through Jealousy or vain glory. God knows whether our heart is kind or mean spirited and whether it is in us to demean others, even as it is His will to bless each of us. "If I regard iniquity in my heart, The Lord will not hear me:" (Psalm 66:18(KJV)

You are bound to receive answers to prayer when you pray according to the Word of God. "Now faith is the substance of things hoped for, the evidence of things not seen." (Hebrews 11:1(KJV) But the only way one can grow in faith is when the Word is imbedded deep within your spirit. Therefore, read and study the Word often and you will find that it will be planted in your spirit. Then you can begin to exercise the Word in faith believing. Try it!

Pray this prayer,

Dear Lord, my desire is to please you, but I know many times I have prayed and not received an answer. Show me how to confidently pray correctly, trusting that I will get an answer. Your Word says we have not because we ask not. Teach me to understand your Word, so that the prayers I pray would be based on your Word every time. Amen!

Or you may need to pray like this,

Father, even as you know my heart, forgive me for my failings. Help me to understand when I am asking amiss. Show me when I only want something because of envy, or the lust of my own flesh. Help me to be satisfied and thankful for your Love and all that you do for me. Thank you for your Grace and Mercy toward me. Father I ask for your direction and instructions to me in how to be of assistance to other persons in need and that I not only lavish your blessings on my family and me. Teach me how to pray in the right way. Thank you for keeping me on the right course. In Jesus Name, AMEN!

Once we understand what God requires of us through His Word, then the understanding will be clear on how to pray in the right way. Over the years, I have heard Television Evangelists say that they have Intercessors praying consistently around the clock, within their churches and homes. Some of these people are paid a salary. Due to the enemy's attacks it is felt, all bases should be covered like the Bible admonishes. The enemy's attacks are fierce, wherein he seeks to intercept the positive action put in place for us via the Holy Spirit through prayer. That is to block the blessing and peacefulness, which God intends for us to enjoy. If one is not a Pastor, there is no need to pay Intercessors as we would not be responsible for a Church. Nevertheless, we are advised to pray without ceasing, as the Bible states. Therefore, with the Holy Spirit's Guidance we can be in Prayer even as we carry out our duties of daily living. Continue to trust Him, even if it may appear you are alone. Believe me, that is when He is most near!

KNOWING GOD
IS WITH YOU

Being the eldest of my siblings, my mom not having access to transportation, was faced with the task of taking me to daycare, after which she walked to work. The only day care center that she said she knew about at that time, was a Government-run Facility called the Cre'che and operated by British Nurses, where working parents could take their little ones. My mom always told me, that she would try to get there on time to collect me in the evenings, so she could continue the long walk home before it got dark. According to her, she would hear babies crying as she approached the building but could pick out my voice among those crying at the same time. I could find you in the dark, she would say.

If a group of moms are in conversation in a room, a baby can easily find his or her mom because they are familiar with her voice. Whether the baby is walking or crawling, they very soon find mom in the crowd. On the other hand, if there was danger or distress and the children are crying, mom could quickly locate where her baby was because she would know her child's voice. How much more can one distinguish the voice of the Lord when He speaks within the spirit, once Jesus is your Savior. John 10:27(KJV) says, "My sheep hear my voice, and I know them, and they follow me:" God's Voice is the one that ultimately matters, when you know Him personally.

Many times people say that they have heard God speak to them, giving them instructions to do or say a particular thing to another person, but usually over the course of a period, if what was spoken does not come to fruition, then that one can be viewed as being untruthful. If someone is arrested as a suspect, or witness to a crime, the Authorities use a lie detector test in order that they may understand the integrity of that witness account. Whether what was said is true or false, if it does not pass the lie detector test, then that account becomes questionable. Even so, when we declare that God said a thing, it should be truth and lining up with the Word of God.

We looked at the importance of Knowing God's Word in an earlier chapter. It is God's desire that we listen for His Voice. As humans we are not always listening, nevertheless, God is always speaking. It is beneficial to us that we seek to hear His Voice in our everyday life. Here are some ways we can hear God speak to us:

1. The more you read through the Bible and study God's Word you grasp it into your spirit. Then you will soon be able to hear His voice clearer. The Lord can speak to you through meditation from study of the Word which you have read. You may have been praying concerning a matter and the Lord could use the same Word to speak an answer to your situation. When the Holy Spirit speaks within our spirit that all is well in a matter and He is bringing you out of a hard situation, believe Him. "For the Word of God is quick, and powerful, and sharper than any two-edged sword, piercing even to the dividing asunder of soul and spirit, and of the joints and marrow, and is a discerner of the thoughts and intents of the heart." (Hebrews 4:12(KJV) The enemy will never encourage you in a positive way. But would use sly tactics to get you to do something negatively that could cause trouble for you. He is never out to help you experience a good outcome.

2. In the stillness of your spirit, you will be able to hear the Lord speak within your spirit. My experience has been that I can hear the Holy Spirit when I am in stillness in my prayer closet. This is when you have made the time to either sit or lie before the Lord, seeking to hear Him. First, honor the Lord audibly with your praises. Let Him know that you love Him and that He alone is Worthy to be praised. After you have poured out your heart in praises, adoration, and worship, tell Him your petitions. Then you must become still before Him. To do this, ask the Holy Spirit to cover your spirit, soul, and body while you wait in silence and stillness to hear Him speak into your spirit.

You may ask, how do you know it is the Holy Spirit speaking to you? You'll know it's Him because God is totally Holy. He will not speak anything evil, vindictive, revengeful, gossip, or malice to you about another, on any situation. He will always prompt you to forgive, love, be patient with others and He'll warn or lead you away from any danger that may be in your way. If unholy thoughts come to you during your time of waiting, then you know that it is the enemy, seeking to double cross the Word from the Lord to you. So, reject and resist the devil's evil tactics. But God is pure, He will not deceive you. Still take your hands off the situation and know that He is working in your favor. God sees you, He knows what you have been going through. If you do not get your answer the first time continue to wait for it. He will speak and you'll be blessed and His Name will be Exalted. "Be still, and know that I am God: I will be exalted among the heathen, I will be exalted in the earth." (Psalm 46:10(KJV)

3. As mentioned before, the Holy Spirit will prompt you if danger is near. Press to be obedient to the leading of the Holy Spirit and when you feel you did not get an answer, then you should wait. I can recall an incident that happened to me

once. I had been planning to travel to the United States for business. About three or four other persons were to also go. But even as I was making plans for the trip, I felt I needed to know that it was within the Lord's will that I travel at that time. Since there would be another meeting just like this one in another few months, my plans never quite agreed with the other persons. But I was also seeking God and wondering why I was not getting a release from The Lord in my spirit. Due to unforeseen circumstances I realized that I would not be on the trip at that time. This was now at least two weeks before the proposed trip, and I had to inform them I would be unable to travel at that time. That seemed to cause a little friction, but my spirit was calm that I had done the right thing.

Two weeks had elapsed, and on the evening when I would have left, a most heart-rending event happened in my family and if I had not been in place someone very dear to me may have lost their life. In fact, at the time of day when this serious incident transpired, in which the Police had to be contacted, I would have been on an airplane headed out of the country, if I had decided to travel without the Holy Spirit's approval. "Declaring the end from the beginning, and from ancient times the things that are not yet done, saying my counsel shall stand, and I will do all my pleasure: (Isaiah 46:10(KJV)." I can only thank God, that He knew what the enemy had planned, and therefore prompted me not to leave the country at that time. I hate to think what might have happened had I not been in my home country. It could only have been that, the enemy's tactics were to cause grave harm to a family member which indeed did happen, but it could have been much worse if no one was there to immediately step in. This person who carried out the attack also suffers from a mental health condition where they become violent when over excited or angry. Danger was indeed facing this family member! "Verily,

verily, I say unto you, He that heareth my Word, and believeth on him that sent me, hath everlasting life, and shall not come into condemnation; but is passed from death unto life (John 5:24(KJV)." Because I did not leave the country, the situation was not extended.

4. When one gets joyful in the things of the Lord, God will give Him the desires of his heart, according to the Word at Psalms 37:4(KJV). But that is easier said than realized for many people. There will always be difficult situations facing us which we need to pray about. The Lord does not wish that we carry around a sad, downcast countenance. It is usually during these times when things are not going so well, that we find it hard to press beyond what we are experiencing. God is pleased when we delight in Him. To delight means to keep a Praise within and a thankful heart, which brings God honor, as we have much to be thankful for. Our joy will indeed be full in Him when we refuse to become fretful about that which only God can make happen or stop some unfortunate situation from happening within our life. Just trust Him!

An unfortunate occurrence could be a domestic matter where a couple is experiencing marriage turmoil. One of them could take action that is humanly natural rather than wait on God. That one through hurt and anger may move out of the marital home, change the locks on the doors, or even remove expensive items, or empty the family bank account. God says simply trust in Him, we are to walk by faith according to the Word. He wants us to completely believe Him. "With all lowliness and meekness, with longsuffering, forbearing one another in love; Endeavoring to keep the unity of the Spirit in the bond of peace. (Ephesians 4:2-3(KJV)." When you stand in faith, God will answer your prayer and you will indeed receive the blessings He's promised.

5. God never contradicts what He has promised, therefore we are to stand on His Word no matter what we see going on around us. A good example of this is when He speaks to us through Philippians 4:19(KJV), "My God shall supply all your need, according to His Riches in Glory by Christ Jesus." When we allow the enemy to whisper to us within our spirit that we will not get answer to prayer; or he may use another person to taunt you that nothing positive is going to happen for you in the foreseeable future. It may be healing from illness, financial success, or even having a good lasting and loving relationship in marriage. God has given us many promises, but when we allow the enemy to plant doubt into our spirit and we believe it, we need to know it is sin on our part, because to disbelieve God is to sin. To study the Word strengthens us and once it is deeply embedded within us, it is easier to understand He means what He says.

Note that the Word says at Luke 21:33(KJV), "Heaven and Earth shall pass away: but My Words shall not pass away." It is comforting and assuring to know that we can grow spiritually to the extent that we are able to hear God's Voice personally. As Christians there are many things to pray about when you are in your prayer closet. There are concerns of where you may feel the direction of your life is headed personally. Naturally you would want to tell your Father God the concerns of your heart, whether it is employment; college for your children; something tangible like a vehicle or home for your family; one may desire a spouse; that family members and colleagues may come to know the Lord.

But know that Satan has also heard you speak to God pouring out your heart's desire, so he begins his evil work of seeking to keep you from receiving God's very best. This makes it most important that one press to walk close to God, knowing His Word and standing on it. So that even if he causes something counterfeit to show up for your life, you would, through the direction of the Holy Spirit, know the difference.

Some ways in which he (the enemy) will surely work is through friends, whom you believe are in your corner supporting you. When friends are sincere, they will pray for you and tell you the t r u t h , when you seem not to make right decisions, even if it hurts. On the other hand, there may be those friends who are either secretly jealous or just mean-spirited and might encourage you to make decisions that are not in keeping with the Word of God. Indeed, they are good manipulators! In choosing friends, we are to trust the Holy Spirit's guidance, that He will reveal when you are around those who care little about the well-being of others. "Ye shall know them by their fruits!" (Matthew 7:16(KJV) "Yea, mine own familiar friend, in whom I trusted, which did eat of my bread, hath lifted up his heel against me." (Psalms 41:9(KJV)

Remain in a spirit of thankfulness because God is a God of many possibilities. You can hear from Him through others, you may be waiting on an answer, and through speaking casually to a family member or a friend, your answer may come out even though you did not reveal what you were going through. The Holy Spirit has many ways in getting an answer to us. Persons have been known to give gifts of money to others for no apparent reason, and those persons have testified that it was the correct amount they were needing at that time. Your Pastor may talk about and bring words of encouragement during his sermon at worship time, and it would be the exact answer to a decision you needed to make, or to get you through what you were going through. Remain open to the Holy Spirit, as there are many possibilities to hearing God speak and act on your behalf. Remember, the enemy has no defense against a seriously focused Believer.

Seeking God's
Best For Life

A child who knows he/she is loved will always feel free to ask mom or dad questions. We are God's children! There is no question or situation concerning our life that our Father God is unable to answer. His answers can always be backed up by His Word, "All scripture is given by inspiration of God, and is profitable for doctrine, for reproof, for correction, for instruction in righteousness: that the man of God may be perfect, thoroughly furnished unto all good works." (2 Timothy 3:16-17(KJV)

You may be concerned about asking God questions. Since I first believed at age 16, up until a few years ago throughout my life as a Christian I have heard it taught and felt myself that one did not ask God just anything. You just said, Lord if it is Thy Will. It was thought of as being rude, untrained and just full of pride, and if you did, such a thing meant you thought of yourself more highly that you should. If you were praying for a vehicle, and if you did get what you were wanting, then you were blessed, and if not, meant that you were either not at the level to receive such a blessing, or God was just not pleased with you at the time and you had to continue to line your life up to be pleasing to Him. When I was young, I would hear older Christians say that, "The young people of today, just don't know how to wait on God."

So, if you did not receive what you were praying for, it meant that you were doing something that displeased God. Take for instance, during this time, I knew of a young couple who did not conceive a child very early on after they were married. They were told by a Pastor that this was God's Will and they should accept it. But they continued to believe somehow that God would allow it to happen for them and after about five years of marriage their child was born. It seems that no one interpreted the Word at John 15:7(KJV), "If ye abide in me, and my words abide in you, ye shall ask what ye will, and it shall be done unto you", to mean exactly what it said, and that you could ask God directly and in Faith believing when you know Him as Father.

At Judges beginning at Chapter 6 through 8 (KJV), the Word speaks of Gideon's account, about asking God questions. An angel appeared to Gideon and told him to break down the Alter of Baal. Even though the people worshipped Baal, they soon understood that Baal had no power, because he could not even protect his own alter from being broken down. But Gideon was still unsure whether God wanted him to free Israel, so his questions were that God would show him signs to verify, whether he was on the right track. The first sign was that a fleece would be left out overnight so that it would gather dew and the ground around it would be dry, the next one was for the fleece to be dry and the ground around it to be wet with dew. After Gideon saw that God answered his questions, he did exactly what God told him. God made him send most of the army back home and he was only to keep 300 good men, which were those who lapped water from their hands rather than bend over and drink. These were the men who won the battle for Israel along with Gideon. "Thus, was Midian subdued before the children of Israel, so that they lifted up their heads no more. And the country was in quietness forty years in the days of Gideon. (Judges 8:28(KJV)"

When God answers our questions it means, we have received a touch of His Favor. We should therefore not take what God does for us lightly. With trust in Him, He's promised to take us through dangers seen and unseen. He promises to restore all that the enemy has stolen and many times gives us much more than we previously owned, while also impressing within us the understanding that we should share with others, some of what He has blessed us with.

David returned to Ziklag (a city of Philistia), where he lived with his 600 men while he was fleeing from King Saul. They learned that the Amalekites had burnt the city and carried off all the wives, their sons and daughters as captives. David along with all the men who were with him wept profusely and David became even more distressed, because the men talked of stoning him. David had no choice but to encourage himself in The Lord his God. He asked The Lord whether he should pursue the Amalekites or not, and would he be successful in overtaking them. "And David enquired at the Lord, saying, shall I pursue after this troop? Shall I overtake them? And he answered him, Pursue: for thou shalt overtake them, and without fail recover all. (1 Samuel 30:8(KJV)"

So it was that David followed the Lord's direction and overtook them, but he only took 400 of the 600 men. The others were too faint, but when it was all over, David made sure the 200 men who could not go any further, received equally just as those who went with him to recover what was taken. In this instance, God was showing David favor and the example here was that, David did not have to measure up and get everything right before God could bless him. Also because of God's favor, David understood to show favor in blessing the 200 men who could not go. He also blessed people in the surrounding towns.

At Matthew 20:1-16(KJV), there is the parable of the owner of a vineyard, who went out one day to hire workers for his vineyard. Those at the first hour agreed to receive one penny, but he hired others at the third, ninth and eleventh hours. At the end of the day all the workers were called to receive their wages beginning with those hired last. When those hired at the first hour also received one penny, they grumbled because they felt they should have received more, forgetting that they had agreed for one penny. In our human nature, many times we believe that our works should be the reason for our success as Christians. Works would be such actions as telling others about God, giving out tracts, teaching Sunday School, helping the poor and going to other areas on Mission. But God looks on the purity of our hearts to be the reason why He blesses us rather than the works we do.

The owner of the vineyard represents Jesus, who accepts everyone into Heaven, regardless of what time you came into God's family. There are no standing ovations or special acknowledgements, on earth to honor those who came in first, or how much works this or any other person was known to have accomplished, even as churches honor persons within their congregation for works they have done. He loves each of us unconditionally which shows that He is preparing us for the Kingdom of God, and it is important to heed His Call and follow the Mandate He has left us with.

Drawing Closer To God Through Prayer

There will always be many voices connected to you seeking to get your attention. Therefore, it is important to have your special time to meet with God daily. You should also know that there is much activity in the spirit world, and Satan's intention is to keep your mind occupied with activities to divert your spirit away from praying and drawing closer to God. The main thing to be aware of is that God is also competing for your spirit, which should rightly belong to Him. That is why it is important to be able to differentiate The Voice of God from that of the enemy, who would do all that he can to distract you while you are in prayer.

One of his tricks would be to remind you of things you may have forgotten to do. Some Christians believe that it is thoughtful to have a note pad handy, so that you may jot down any thoughts that may come to mind, which you can take care of later. If you have done this before, please take note of how many things you would have jotted down after your time with God. Did the notes on your pad reflect revelations, or directions from HIM? Were they of an every-day nature of things to do? The enemy would make sure to remind you of many things which you should be taking care of, and when you really examine, these would be things you would have done in any event, such as: Call your mother; Take the clothes to the cleaners; Did you cut the stove off; Speak to your boss about the matter at the office; Check the children's homework; Call the repairman to fix something at the house; Something you need to take care of for church etc. I have tried this before, but the only things that kept coming into my spirit were reminders of normal things of life that I would have taken care of in any event. This method cannot work if you are seeking a deeper relationship with God.

These are all important things that need to be taken care of, but with trust in the Holy Spirit who walks alongside us, while also living within us, He will surely bring all things to our minds that we need to remember at the right time, so let's trust Him. Another way to help oneself, is to keep a prepared list of immediate things to be done prior to our prayer time (like turning the stove off) and after our time with God (like checking the children's homework). The enemy knows he cannot get us to stop praying, but what he does is to try to make sure we get very little traction or grow deeper in the Holy Spirit, or any answers from God because if he continues reminding us of the normal happenings of life at prayer time, causing us to lose focus or distracting us from the main purpose of being in our Father God's presence and hearing from Him, he believes he would have won.

You will know when you've heard from God, when He tells you to do something positive, which can be like doing something good for a disadvantaged family; praying for the person in the cubicle next to you at work, rather than disliking that one in your spirit; or donating money to a much needed charity at church or in your community. When He speaks in this way, you have no choice but to write it down, as you know it is something you had never thought of before.

Knowing God's Word, Meditation on the Word and Continual Prayer are areas that are most important. The enemy cannot get a serious believer to quit pressing into God with the aid of the Holy Spirit, but he will try to keep one's mind distracted such as, the constant ringing of the telephone; family activities etc. thus making it difficult to remain focused. One's mind can easily wander while a word relevant to our spiritual growth is being spoken, whether at church, or otherwise in our hearing that could mean spiritual life for us and reveal to us how to get help in areas where we need to be free, either to help ourselves or someone close to us. Christians can very easily get caught up in that which is not godly such as idle conversations and speaking ungodly jokes which are not grounded in the Word.

It is important not to view the shortcomings of others or portray them in a negative way by making oneself appear superior. Surely this is not a good attitude in the face of God as He loves all his children and each person has strengths and weaknesses within. This can be condemning as others always know more about us than we think they do. These can be hindrances orchestrated by the enemy to slow down our spiritual growth, and the opening of our eyes in spirit. Let us also be careful that interactions with others are the best, as our attitude can be the means whether someone else does not stumble in their walk before God, people always know when one is faking it. Words spoken are important to those around us and it makes a difference whether they give their heart to the Lord, or even remain a Christian if they are in a spiritually weakened state from life's experiences and therefore becomes hurt by what has been said. Our lives are an open book for others to view. "Even so, the tongue is a little member, and boasteth great things. Behold, how great a matter a little fire kindleth! And the tongue is a fire, a world of iniquity: so is the tongue among our members, that it defileth the whole body, and sets on fire the course of nature; and it is set on fire of hell." (James 3:5, 6(KJV)

A good father loves his children and acts to protect them if someone else harms or bullies them. As earthly parents, we can say Amen to that. God, our Father loves His children and would protect them if they are in danger or harmed. As people of God, let's live pure before Him, so as not to hinder our own prayers being answered and we can hear Him clearly speak into our spirit. Let's keep our prayer line clear to hear Him.

This Old Time Gospel Song comes to mind,

TELEPHONE TO GLORY

Telephone to Glory, Oh what Joy Divine!
I can feel the current moving on the line.
Made by God The Father for his very own,
You may talk to Jesus on this Royal Telephone.

Central's never busy, always on the line,
You can hear from Heaven, always anytime.
Tis a Royal Service, Built for one and all.
When you get in trouble, give this Royal Line a call.

There will be no charges, telephone is free.
It was built for service, just for you and me.
There will be no waiting on this Royal Line,
Telephone to Glory always answers just on time.

By: Frederick M. Lehman
https//hymnary.org/text/centrals-never-busy-always-on-the-line

This is an old Gospel Song which started in the United States. I grew up 'belting it out' along with the radio always just singing along, even as I was not sure if these were the exact words. It tells of a true message of prayer and we get it. It means, we can always contact Heaven and talk with God, as He always waits to hear us. The writer of this song certainly got the lyrics from God. But sometimes we allow our clear line to get crossed through our own ignorance. Let's be wise and keep our line clear to God. I grew up hearing this song on the radio and singing along. But not until I accepted Jesus as Savior, did I understand exactly what the lyrics truly meant.

We talked about only a few of the obstacles that can hinder a Christian's prayer life. Here are some important ways in which we can get a growing and meaningful spirit-filled prayer life, which can bring us to more victorious living, and will bring us to the great opportunity of knowing and experiencing a more intimate relationship with Holy Spirit. There is a need to be alone during your special time with God. Group prayer and family worship are important and have their places, but time spent alone with God is most beneficial to every individual child of God.

It is crucial that when you go into your Prayer closet, the first thing one should do is thank Holy Spirit for His presence for allowing you to come before Him, then for His love for you. Then we should Worship God with our whole being. One can sing worship songs or play tapes. But also remember, God wants to hear our voice in worship to Him. He is most Worthy, so give Him His due. Thank Him for all He does and will do for you. **Honor Him!** The Bible tells us that God inhabits the praises of His people. He loves when we Praise and Worship Him, and we are blessed by doing so. Then we go before God in prayer in Jesus' Name.

My personal experience has been, that after I have sung, praised and prayed to God in Jesus' Name, I never just jump up and leave the prayer closet to continue my busy schedule. It is wise to get quiet before Him and ask Him to rid your mind of distractions and other thoughts. You will find that He will do it right away. Quietly wait on God for a few minutes in the first instance, until you have learned to wait longer, as He is always speaking, and He will speak to you within your spirit. Have patience, if you were not successful in hearing today, you will eventually hear Him speak directly to you. You would know that it is the Lord Who has spoken, because that word will resonate within you and you will know it is God, as you could not have possibly thought what He'll say in your natural mind. God is Holy and Pure, He will not speak to you in a self-serving manner and will never cause you to harbor jealousy of another or tell you anything mean or untoward to do or speak to anyone, He's not a frivolous trouble maker. He is our Righteous Father God and Worthy of all Honor and Praise. Always Praise Him within your spirit!

Seek the Presence of the Holy Spirit. His Spirit is sensitive, so do not get prideful, about how long you prayed in your prayer language and how spiritually deep you are. He knows when His children are prideful, so seek to be humble before Him, all Power belongs to Him and He gives it to whomever He Wills. It also causes you to remain humble when you are interacting with others. "God hath spoken once; twice have I heard this; that power belongeth unto God, (Psalm 62:11(KJV)." Continue to build your prayer life and remain in the study of The Word. It teaches you to walk in a spiritually mature and godly manner, shunning negativity or that which is unholy which would harm your successful spiritual growth. The enemy's plight is to weaken your witness in the earth.

The Enemy's Efforts To Use Each One For His Purpose

The tactics of the adversary is to ensure that we **take offence** in any way he can get us to in an effort to hinder our peace within and spiritual progress before God. If he fails in separating families, then he would try to make it difficult for us at work, school, church or wherever people gather. Offence touches everyone, weather wealthy or living in poverty, you have been offended at some point in life. There is no respect of persons in doing wrong because the enemy is fierce in his endeavors in plotting to cause you to fail in your walk with God. He does it by causing you to become offended either by something someone said or did toward you. Sometimes we may be able to brush off little brash things that people say or do, or we may be so hurt that it can go on for many years and we find ourselves not speaking to the one whom we believe offended us. Persons have been known to separate from families because of what might have happened. The Bible says, "Woe unto the world because of offences! For it must needs be that offences come; but woe to that man by whom the offence cometh! (Matthew 18:7(KJV)"

We can also be guilty of offending others, so offence can happen both ways and when we know we have hurt someone be quick to apologize and make it right. The enemy works in our minds to sway us toward any negativity that we are open to and fight against each other. Let us not keep records of the wrong someone else has done to us and keep replaying the old broken record. Even if they do not offer an apology, forgive them in any event. We would know we have truly forgiven and let it go when we do not feel the need to rehearse the pain again and again. It is then when we will begin to heal from the hurt. The Word says, "Keep thy heart with all diligence; for out of it, are the issues of life. (Proverbs 4:23(KJV)" Let us be vigilant over our own hearts! God rewards us when we press to let go of offences and walk in love. God has not forgotten you and knows exactly what you have endured. So, we do not have to wait around to see if they get what is coming to them. It is not healthy to walk in offence as it only hurts more and can lead to other conditions such as Depression or Anxiety.

Now that you walk with God, trust that He will prompt you when you have taken offence and become hurt for any reason. My experiences have been that, offences constantly come at you, as you will soon find out. You may go into a store, and somebody does or says something negative or rude to you. You go to work or to a meeting and an offence happens, even in the parking lot something may go wrong to upset your spirit and put you off course. It may not have even been intentional, or you might have had a rough day, and could have taken what another person said out of context. One does not seek to be offended, but the enemy makes sure offences are presented to you. Ask God to show you when an offence has occurred, to give you an opportunity to forgive that one in your heart and to never show any ill will toward them. **Do Not take the bait!**

We must depend on God for spiritual strength, to help us overcome when we have been offended. Offences are designed by the enemy to cause anger within you. He does this by putting mischief in the minds of others to carry out the offence, even possibly unknowing to them. Never seek revenge or try to repay in the manner of the wrong which was done. "Not rendering evil for evil, or railing for railing:

but contrariwise blessing; knowing that ye are thereunto called, that ye should inherit a blessing. (1 Peter 3:9(KJV)" For instance, if it is felt your name has been slandered, then one should not also seek to slander that person's name, which is not godly and causes more friction. Sometimes persons do not know that they have hurt you. Or they may know and do not really care. Staying away from gossip and tale-baring is important, as the Holy Spirit is the best revealer of character. Trust Him to reveal who is the new person at work, church, the neighborhood etc. and He does not tell lies. The important thing is that if one is faking good character, they can only pretend for so long. "Casting down imaginations, and every high thing that exalteth itself against the knowledge of God, and bringing into captivity every thought to the obedience of Christ:" (2 Corinthians 10:5(KJV) Again, don't take the enemy's bait!

One should notice that in each of the above situations, un-forgiveness, holding grudges, bitterness, anger, resentment, strife and contention, jealousy and envy, gossip, lying, judging, pride, adversity, panic and fear etc. are all negative states of the spirit. It means any of these occur within us and cannot be seen with the physical eye. It also reveals that the enemy does his best, to fill our spirit with the negative, to weaken, intimidate, cause insecurity and to keep us from fulfilling the purpose God sent us to the earth to fulfill. One can become so preoccupied trying to get over what they believe has been done personally toward them that they discontinue seeking spiritual growth or moving forward in life. Many become stunted in general and like the old dog – always chasing after its tail, going nowhere.

In order to overcome depressing situations like those above, it is very important to reject the adversary, the enemy, the devil, Satan. Now how does one reject Satan, you may ask?

Understand that Satan is a liar, and the father of lies. The truth cannot be found in him. Do you want a liar speaking into your spirit, controlling your mind? (John 8:44(KJV)

Do not yield to temptation and allow false imaginations into your spirit. Remember, he seduced Adam and Eve and God had to expel them from their home in the Garden of Eden.... (Genesis 3(KJV). Pray and ask the Lord, what He says about a situation you may be going through. Be assured that He will answer you and will never tell you to do anything evil to anyone, but to continue praying for that one that the scales be removed from their eyes, and turn their life around. God will bless you indeed!

Jesus (God's Son) was taken up into a mountain, where Satan tried to seduce Him to throw Himself down, promising he would give Him all the kingdoms if Jesus would only, fall down and worship him. Jesus had to rebuke Satan by telling him that, it is written "Thou shalt worship the Lord thy God, and Him only shalt thou serve." (Matthew 4:10(KJV)

We need to understand that many of Satan's attacks begin in the mind, therefore we can also rebuke him from our spirit. When you get thoughts that you know you could not have thought, just speak to your own spirit. Say to him speaking through your mind – **Satan I resist you, leave now in Jesus Name.** Once you say in Jesus Name, he must flee. God has given you the power to resist him and overcome. Do not begin to panic, he is helpless when you call on Jesus' Name, and he must leave. You may be in a meeting or in church, or entertaining company at home and you do not have to appear silly by blurting out 'In the Name of Jesus', and others around you believe that you are losing your mind. If he attacks you in the mind resist him the same way when you are around others.

You will find, he will indeed stop harassing you immediately, but he will try to do it again for several times, till eventually he will understand you mean what you say, as God has given you the power to resist him. "Submit yourselves therefore to God. Resist the devil, and he will flee from you (James 4:7(KJV)." We all struggle against evil forces sent by Satan to gain traction in our lives to depress by causing us to carry offence. He works in the mind, thus interfering with and seeking to alter our clean thinking. When Satan brings thoughts, which you know you did not think on your own, resist by telling him, 'I resist you in the name of Jesus'. He is an intruder and not welcome in your spirit. This is how he gains access to you through the mind and plots to not only destroy your relationships but aims to destroy you shutting down the accomplishing of your purpose in the earth, as you cannot successfully move forward, inwardly holding ill-will toward others.

In his efforts to carry out evil in the earth, Satan needs to occupy a human body, which means he would have to inhabit his target through the mind. Once he is successful in changing the mind to go in the direction he wants, he then knows he has won over on you to do his bidding. Always remember when you feel yourself being pressured by the enemy, just submit to the presence of God, and he will flee from you. His direction is always evil, and his purpose is to not only destroy the one being targeted, but also the body being used to commit the offence, which could be you. It's why you have got to resist him because he is completely evil! He does not like to see humans agreeing together and fellowshipping, whether it's at church, home, work, school or anywhere else.

Think of two friends who have become best friends and share important information about family plans and what their endeavors are. Then another friend who is not as close to either of them, becomes jealous and begins to secretly tell tales (lies) back and forth from one to the other, without either one knowing. Then one friend begins to believe the other was being a hypocrite, naturally that friendship may not last, unless either or both see the situation for what it is and rebuke the enemy. "And I heard a loud voice saying in heaven, Now is come salvation and strength, and the kingdom of our God, and the power of his Christ: for the accuser of our brethren is cast down, which accused them before our God day and night (Revelation 12:10(KJV)." Satan is the accuser of the brethren and will always seek to put your life in turmoil. This is how he accused Job, through his friends who said that God was punishing Job because he had sinned against God.

Satan seeks to work through the minds of every human on the earth, so through their thinking, orchestrated by the enemy, criminals commit crimes which include heinous acts - theft, rapes, murders and other evils to put it lightly. This is how many of them are caught, because after the act, the enemy leaves them and they then realize the evil they have done, many of them take their own lives, because they have no power to resist the enemy and sin has caught up with them.

As Christians, we are to "Put on the whole armor of God that ye may be able to stand against the wiles of the devil. For we wrestle not against flesh and blood, but against principalities, against powers, against the rulers of the darkness of this world, against spiritual wickedness in high places (Ephesians 6:11-12(KJV)." This means that once we are dressed in the full armor of God, it will not be easy for the enemy to win over on us, even as his evil forces try, they will eventually stop. We therefore should resist him every time when he seeks to torment on a situation. It is best that believers know and study this whole passage of Ephesians 6:10-18(KJV), as it is a guide in knowing that the enemy seeks to attack us from every area of the armor.

Satan is not a harmless spirit, but we have all heard many people jokingly say, stop blaming everything on the devil. I once heard a Pastor say that the devil did not cause the friction that was going on in his Church at the time, it was those so-called wicked ones, who call themselves Saints. He said he knew that people made the devil cry because they blamed everything on him. Listen friends, the devil is a crafty, subtle, evil demon, full of guile and is out to destroy God's people because he was thrown out of Heaven. Know that Satan is a defeated foe, and he has no inkling how to speak the truth. By the way, I hope that Pastor has now realized that it was the devil that caused the unrest, and those persons whom he may have physically observed conducting the unrest in his church, were those who allowed Satan's evil forces, the enemy to work through them. They were being used and did not understand how to resist the evil one, either because they did not listen to the Holy Spirit, or they were not taught how to resist him.

The reason Jesus came to earth was to give His Life to redeem us back to God and to give us the right to go to Heaven through Salvation. "For God so loved the world, that He gave His only begotten Son, that whosoever believeth in Him should not perish, but have everlasting life." (John 3:16(KJV) Resist Satan's evil tactics '**In the name of Jesus**', beginning today! He studies each human from birth, and believes he knows how to ensnare each with his many evil plans and tactics. On accepting Jesus as Savior, we are immediately made the righteousness of God in Christ Jesus, and He, Jesus, becomes our Elder Brother as God is our Father, Hebrews 2:11(KJV). Therefore, we need to seek God for His direction in all things, meaning we need God's wisdom how to pray, how to conduct ourselves even when we're alone, not allowing our minds to wander off through lust, anger, nursing unforgiveness in our heart toward those whom we feel have hurt us, living in fear and whatever else he can conjure up to come at us with. But God has promised us relief from the enemy. "If any man lacks wisdom, let him ask of God who gives liberally, and upbraideth not; and it shall be given him (James 1:5(KJV)." That means He does not hold wisdom from you, but He expects that you ask for it, "In Jesus Name".

You may not realize it, but the enemy knows that if you are here on the earth today God has a great Plan that He's sent you to the earth to accomplish. There are also amazing promises that are already listed in the Bible for you. Hold fast to God, pray continually for those whom you know have been lied to by the devil. Then forgive them for causing you frustration and pain, or whatever evil he has orchestrated in trying to make your life a living hell. Be encouraged that The Holy Spirit will help you successfully overcome every friction in your life, through prayer and trust, In Jesus Name. What will set you back, is if you take offence and allow it to cause bitterness within your spirit.

Just as Satan uses others to attack and hurt us, he seeks to use us to attack others, when we do not put on the whole armor of God. Do not take revenge, he knows taking revenge will push us further on a path which we do not wish to be on. We should be vigilant over our own minds and watch our attitude and deportment in our interactions. As pointed out previously, everyone experiences turmoil orchestrated by the enemy. Now along with all the other tactics from the enemy, the adversary is trying to bring you down, watches your every move and has been doing so since your birth. He notes your mistakes and wrongs, your preferences in every area of your life and continually bombards you about what you should be doing in an effort, to bring guilt and shame upon you. "For your shame ye shall have double; and for confusion they shall rejoice in their portion: therefore in their land they shall possess the double: everlasting joy shall be unto them (Isaiah 61:7(KJV)." He always seeks to pit one person against another to cause confusion among any group of people in order to keep confusion and contention alive.

God has also watched you from birth, and He knows not only your capabilities, but your every nuance, and would not have given you a mandate if He felt you were not capable. When friction happens in your life it is just to get you side-tracked. Re-gain your focus and like the Apostle Paul say, "I press toward the mark for the prize of the high calling of God in Christ Jesus (Philippians 3:14)." Therefore, let us hold others in high esteem as we trust God to let us know the truth about persons we do not know, rather than believing any evil we have heard concerning that one which may be untrue. "Let nothing be done through strife or vain glory; but in lowliness of mind let each esteem other better than themselves (Philippians 2:3(KJV)." When we rely on the Holy Spirit, He will reveal who each person is.

He (the devil) will tell you, 'see there,' God is not pleased with you because you did so and so, or said this or that, or showed a nasty attitude because of what they said about you. You're saved, aren't you? He'll say, you can't live a Christian life, you make too many mistakes,

God doesn't want you. When this happens, and it will, remind Satan that **you have been justified by God**. Since he speaks fear and doubt to you in your spirit, resist him in your spirit. Say, **"I resist you Satan In the Name of Jesus."** God has forgiven you of your sins and you have been vindicated. Knowing that Prayer and Thanksgiving to God in Jesus Name, gives you the power that you need to overcome and make the devil flee from bombarding your mind. When he does that, he wants you to stop moving forward.

Because Satan's job is to seek to get Christians to fail, so that he can accuse them before God, our job is to prove him false, by trusting in the Lord through the strength of the Holy Spirit walking alongside and living within you. Be vigilant over your own Spirit, Soul, and Body so that the enemy does not gain any traction in your life. Satan does not care that you have a Testimony or how long you have been a Born Again Christian, he just does not want you to be successful. He will therefore try his best to defeat you, so that your witness and Ministry to others is fruitless. Stay on the right course through the strength of the Holy Spirit. Let us pray:

> Father, thank you for bringing me to this point in my Christian Walk with you. Teach me to know and understand, when I am being attacked by the enemy and his evil forces, through the Wisdom which you are imparting into my spirit right now and show me how to believe your Word and resist the tactics of the enemy every time. Therefore, I stand on the power of Your Word, and Thank you for giving me the strength to stand on Your Holy Authority. "In the Name of Jesus." Amen!

Pray in the above manner every time you need to.

WHO IS THE
HOLY SPIRIT?

The Holy Spirit or the Holy Ghost, as He is often referred to, is the Third Person of The Trinity, The Father, The Son (Jesus) and The Holy Spirit. His name alone says to us, He is Holy, and naturally exhibits the Spirit of Holiness, always Glorifying Jesus. "These things have I spoken unto you, being yet present with you. But the Comforter, which is the Holy Ghost, whom The Father will send in my name, He shall teach you all things and bring all things to your remembrance, whatsoever I have said unto you." (John 14:25, 26(KJV) He is Teacher, Comforter and Advocate walking alongside and staying with us to help and guide us into truth. Before you became a Christian, God the Father drew you to Him through convicting you within your own spirit, John 6:44(KJV). After we are convicted, Jesus saves us from sin through Salvation, John 3:16(KJV). He clarifies to us who Jesus is as Savior. Now let us understand more about Him. The Holy Spirit bears witness of Jesus in the earth. His attributes are:

Eternal – He will be your Counsellor and remain with you forever to impart knowledge and Grace to you. "How much more shall the Blood of Christ, who through the eternal Spirit offered Himself without spot to God, purge your conscience from dead works to serve the living God?" (Hebrews 9:14(KJV)

Omnipresent, He's ever with us, never leaving or forsaking us. David again tells God, "Whither shall I go from thy Spirit? Or whither shall I flee from thy presence? If I ascend up into Heaven, thou art there: if I make my bed in hell, behold thou art there." (Psalm 139:7-8(KJV)

Omnipotent, God is Almighty, all Powerful, meaning He knows everything. Before you ask Him a question, He has the answer to every query, God was there before the Creation. "And the earth was without form, and void; and darkness was upon the face of the deep, and the Spirit of God moved upon the face of the waters. And God said, "Let there be light, and there was light." (Genesis 1:2-3(KJV); Job declared, "The Spirit of God has made me, and the breath of the Almighty has given me life." (Job 33:4(KJV)

When we repented of our sins and became a Christian, the Holy Spirit came in at that time, He therefore, empowers us to live the Christian life because He now lives within us. After we accept Jesus as Personal Savior, the Holy Spirit within gives us a desire to live clean and holy, doing good things moving away from that which we previously did that was wrong, which we know did not please the Lord. This is our first encounter with the Holy Spirit. Many Christians can live a born-again life for the remainder of their days on earth and still go to Heaven. But there are deeper depts provided by God to us as members of His Family, and that is deeper depts of the Holy Spirit. This comes with the gift of Speaking in Tongues. This helps us to do a greater work in exercising the Gifts of The Holy Spirit for The Kingdom of God.

Through His great Love and Mercy, God has given us the Power of the Holy Spirit, who also lives within us. Many Christians also have this gift of the Holy Spirit with the evidence of Speaking in Tongues, which is supernatural and given by God on the Day of Pentecost. "And when the day of Pentecost was fully come, they were all with one accord in one place. And suddenly there came a sound from Heaven as of a rushing mighty wind, and it filled all the house where they were sitting. And there appeared unto them cloven tongues like as of fire, and it sat upon each of them. And they were all filled with the Holy Ghost, and began to speak with other tongues, as the Spirit gave them utterance." (Acts 2:1-4(KJV)

The Chapter in Acts does not tell us that the one hundred and twenty were planning to receive anything from God, except that they may have been praying for the way forward after all that had happened. But we are told that they were all with one accord in the same place. Therefore, they were all in agreement together as they waited on God. Then God blessed them with the showering of the Holy Spirit with the utterance of speaking in tongues. Even as you are filled with the Spirit when you accepted Christ into your heart, we should continually ask God for His guidance in doing those things He wants us to do. "I will not leave you comfortless: I will come to you". (John 14:18(KJV) So God came to His people on the Day of Pentecost.

The Holy Spirit with the evidence of speaking in tongues gives the assurance that God is hearing us and know we are there. I personally began to speak in tongues while at home laying on my living room floor pouring the issues and fears of my heart and life out to God and crying, all washed in tears because I felt I was going through so very much. Then my English turned into another language. I did not know at the time that it was called the 'prayer language' and my soul longed for it. The Lord was praying supernaturally through me and imparting peace within my spirit at the same time. Now I'm not saying everyone's experience should be exactly like mine. But I am saying, that if you know in your heart you wish the gift of speaking and praying in tongues, sincerely ask the Lord for it, believing by Faith that it is done, and He will shower you with it. Then don't be afraid and begin to speak right away. Do not try to form your own words through your intellect, let the words come and even though they may not make sense, you are speaking in tongues. Now speak every day, and you will begin to speak with fluency.

Everyone can receive the gift of tongues, and through faith just tell the Holy Spirit to fill you with the gift of tongues. Then begin to speak and I can tell you, the unknown language will come from your lips. You will not have to practice or fight for it. Now you may only receive a few words at first, but after you speak in tongues every day, you will become fluent. Speaking in tongues should not be looked on as a badge or to be worn with an ego. The minute we become puffed up, we can understand right away, that this will not be from the Holy Spirit. The gift of tongues is to comfort and protect, impart understanding, make things plain to you, the Holy Spirit is your teacher. He is the one to guide you when you are going the wrong way, and helps you make those decisions that you could not make with your natural understanding. You are not a normal person anymore, you belong to God. "But the natural man receives not the things of the Spirit of God: for they are foolishness unto him: neither can he know them, because they are spiritually discerned" (1 Corinthians 2:14). To pray in tongues, means that you are praying truth, the exact prayer you should be praying. Not having to prepare what to say in your mind is vital and builds your faith that you will receive answers to prayer.

Some ways the Holy Spirit imparts the gifts of tongues to believers:

1. Speaking in tongues is a private prayer language to build up prayer and praise to God in us. "Likewise the Spirit also helpeth our infirmities: for we know not what we should pray for as we ought: but the Spirit itself maketh intercession for us with groanings which cannot be uttered." (Romans 8:26(KJV)

2. Tongues is a supernatural sign that the Holy Spirit uses through Preachers other Believers and those sharing the gospel like missionaries and Evangelists etc., to get unbelievers to see God's Love. "And these signs shall follow them that believe; in my name shall they cast out devils; they shall speak with new tongues;" (Mark 16:17(KJV)

3. For the building up of the Body of Christ. Through prophecy and interpretation. "If any man speaks in an unknown tongue, let it be by two, or at the most by three, and that by course; and let one interpret." (1 Corinthians 14:27(KJV)

When we do not allow evidence of the presence of the Holy Spirit to be seen in us and is embarrassed to let colleagues and friends know we're now Christian, we quench God's Spirit within, choosing to live outside of His example. "Quench not the Spirit." (Thessalonians 5:19(KJV)

Believers can very easily be indifferent to The Holy Spirit. That is, persons may lie to him, as Ananias and his wife did, when they lied to Peter about the price of the land they sold. "But Peter said, Ananias, why hath Satan filled your heart to lie to the Holy Ghost, and to keep back part of the price of the land?" (Acts 5:3 – 11(KJV) We can also grieve the Holy Spirit, i.e. being disobedient to what the Word of God says, by walking in pride rather than humility and not heeding His warnings when He seeks to shield us from trouble. "And grieve not the Holy Spirit of God, whereby ye are sealed unto the day of redemption." (Ephesians 4:30(KJV)

You can trust The Holy Spirit with your deepest secrets, even though He already knows. He is more loyal than your closest friend and He reveals to your conscience when you have sinned. Your friend may be afraid to lose your friendship, or may only see what your actions are, when you are physically with them, but the Holy Spirit sees the intents of the heart. He prompts and even impresses upon us, when we need to repent, and be aware when we're not making the right decisions, because He lives in us. "All the ways of a man are clean in his own eyes; but the Lord weigheth the spirits (Proverbs 16:2(KJV)." The Holy Spirit helps us to live a clean life in our Spirit, Soul and Body, which includes our thoughts. Now He is unable to keep us from returning to sin because God has given us the will-power to make our own decisions. He is our helper in times of need and will prompt us if we are about to do something that does not represent Christ. We are unable to overcome sin by human nature only and must trust the Holy Spirit. The Holy Spirit longs for us to trust Him so He can help us. "Let your conversation be without covetousness; and be content with such things as ye have: for He hath said, I will never leave thee, nor forsake thee. That we may boldly say, The Lord is my helper, and I will not fear what man shall do unto me." (Hebrews 13:5,6(KJV)

Romans 8:14(KJV), "For as many as are led by the Spirit of God, they are the sons of God." This is the work of the Holy Spirit in us, He is God in us after we are saved from sin. Jesus is Immanuel, God with us. This establishes that both The Holy Spirit and Jesus Are God. It is most important that you listen to the Voice of The Holy Spirit, who waits to guide and walk alongside you to keep you on the right course.

The Baptism of The Holy Spirit will give you the power to overcome obstacles and temptations that the adversary seeks to confront you with. Know that the power of The Holy Spirit is within you. This means that you have the power to pray for the sick, and they will be healed. When you receive the Holy Spirit within, you carry the same power as the Apostles Paul and the other Apostles in the New Testament and even in these modern times there are those who walk in the Gifts of the Spirit. But before we talk about the gifts of the Spirit, here are some of the ways the Holy Spirit helps us.

He's Comforter, helping us in times of sorrow or distress, that is, whatever happens in your life that may negatively impact you. He strengthens us when we are feeling overwhelmed by giving us the confidence we need, at just the right time. He is also there to prompt us through His Words of Wisdom when not to become involved in matters that can cause us trouble. "And I will pray the Father, and he shall give you another Comforter, that he may abide with you forever. Even the Spirit of truth; whom the world cannot receive. Because it seeth him not, neither knoweth him, but ye know him, for he dwelleth with you, and shall be in you. I will not leave you comfortless: I will come to you. (John 14:16-18(KJV)"

Advocate, always pleading our case and our cause to God when we're in trouble. An advocate is one who stands for someone to act and testify on their behalf, thus causing you to win cases against you. The Holy Spirit (God on the earth). "But the Comforter, which is the Holy Ghost, whom the Father will send in my name, he shall teach you all things, and bring all things to your remembrance, whatsoever I have said unto you. (John 14:26(KJV)"

Intercessor – One who stands in the gap and intercedes for us, when we do not know how to pray, He gives us the right words within our spirit, so we can stay on the right course. He also prompts us to pray at the right time, e.g. if a family member is in trouble, if danger is near, because in our humanity alone we would never know these things. "Likewise the Spirit also helpeth our infirmities: for we know not what we should pray for as we ought: but the spirit itself maketh intercession for us with groanings which cannot be uttered. (Romans 8:26(KJV)"

Teacher – God has given us a gift to teach, which begins within. The Holy Spirit will teach us those things which we do not know or understand. He gives wisdom through Faith in Him. "But the Comforter, which is the Holy Ghost, whom the Father will send in my name, He shall teach you all things, and bring all things to your remembrance, whatsoever I have said unto you." (John 14:26(KJV)

He Guides us – Let us allow the Holy Spirit to guide us. It may be one is seeking to purchasing a home, the type of investment to make, seeking employment, deciding on which college to attend etc. Whatever the concern or need for your life, He wants to be a part, and is willing to guide. "For as many as are led by the Spirit of God, they are the sons of God." (Romans 8:14); "Howbeit when he, the Spirit of Truth is come, He will guide you into all the truth: for He shall not speak of Himself; but whatsoever He shall hear, that shall He speak: and He will show you things to come" (John 16:13(KJV)

Stands-by Us – He intervenes when we cannot handle a situation, whether we are ill, or otherwise, and in times of weakness, He comes alongside us. "But if the Spirit of him that raised up Jesus from the dead dwell in you, he that raised up Christ from the dead shall also quicken your mortal bodies by the Spirit that dwells in you." (Romans 8:11(KJV)

He's Counselor – Gives advice guidance and direction in our everyday lives and directs us which scriptures in God's Word to stand on in every situation. "All scripture is given by inspiration of God, and is profitable for doctrine, for reproof, for correction, for instruction in righteousness." (2 Timothy 3:16(KJV)

Revealer of the Truth – When we are seeking an answer from God on a matter, or there can even be one around us, who is pretending to be a friend, with Faith in Him, the Holy Spirit reveals the answer, and when danger is near. The Holy Spirit speaks for Jesus. "Howbeit when he, the spirit of truth, is come, he will guide you into all truth: for he shall not speak of himself; but whatsoever he shall hear, that shall he speak: and he will show you things to come. (John 16:13)"

GIFTS OF THE HOLY SPIRIT

The nine gifts of the Holy Spirit found in 1 Corinthians 12:8, are divided into three categories, (1) Gifts of Revelation; Word of Wisdom, Word of Knowledge, Discerning of Spirits. (2) Inspirational Gifts; Prophecy, Tongues, Interpretation of Tongues. (3) Gifts of Power; Faith, The Gift of Healing, The Working of Miracles. God has given the Gifts for the uplifting and encouragement of the Body of Christ and He gives supernatural abilities to each as He deems necessary. All demonstrations of the gifts of the Holy Spirit would come from God, through the one speaking, and should be in accordance with the Word of God.

Word of Wisdom - Psalm 111:10(KJV) says, "The Fear of The Lord is the beginning of Wisdom: A good understanding have all they that do His Commandments: His Praise endureth forever." The fear spoken of in this verse, is to have much reverence for God and to be obedient in seeking to do His Will in loving and understanding others. When one abides in communion with God, it becomes easier to impart a Word of Wisdom **directly from the heart** and not from our personal thinking, hence revealing His Will and Purpose. The Holy Spirit intervenes into hard situations that would otherwise be difficult to solve. The Word of Wisdom is meant to bring blessing, prosperity, and healing others. "But the natural man receiveth not the things of the spirit of God: for they are foolishness to him: neither can he know them, because they are spiritually discerned." (1 Corinthians 14(KJV) These are the deep things of God!

Word of Knowledge - The spirit of discernment is the knowledge and understanding of God's Will for your life and the lives of others. Knowing God's Word and understanding whether that which is being said to you is truthful, God has said it, and it came directly from His Mind. The gift of Word of knowledge is important in the life of a Christian as it **helps one to understand if something is of God or not**, and how to shun evil. "Beloved, believe not every spirit, but try the spirits whether they are of God: because many false prophets are gone out into the world (1 John 4:1(KJV)." There are indeed persons within the body of Christ, who claim to speak for God but are deceitful, disguising themselves as sincere and inwardly are wolves in sheep's clothing.

Discerning of Spirits – God gives His people the Gift of Discerning of Spirits, where a message coming from God via the Holy Spirit should **coincide with the Word of God**. Discernment of Spirits reveal whether the person is speaking from **God**, or the **devil**. "Now the God of patience and consolation grant you to be likeminded one toward another according to Christ Jesus: That ye may with one mind and one mouth glorify God, even the Father of our Lord Jesus Christ. (Romans 15:5-6(KJV)" Knowing God's Word is key to understanding when someone is not being honest and speaking from an evil spirit and the devil. "But exhort one another daily, while it is called today, lest any of you be hardened through the deceitfulness of sin. (Hebrews 3:13(KJV)"

This reveals when spirits not from Him are operating through a person who is bringing a message. It also brings to light that spirits not from God can operate with false motives through people. "And it came to pass as we went to prayer, a certain damsel possessed with a spirit of divination met us, which brought her masters much gain by soothsaying: The same followed Paul and us, and cried, saying, These men are the servants of the most high God, which shew unto us the way of salvation and this did she many days. But Paul, being grieved turned and said to the spirit, I command thee in the name of Jesus Christ to come out of her. And he came out the same hour. **This damsel was speaking through a spirit from the devil.** (Acts 16:16-18(KJV)" Also, Ananias and his wife Sapphira decided together to lie and conceal the amount of money they received from the sale of property which they had no reason to, as it all belonged to them. Their decision was to keep part of the proceeds for themselves, so they brought a portion of the money, putting it down before Peter at his feet. "But Peter said, Ananias, why hath Satan filled thine heart to lie to the Holy Ghost, and to keep back part of the price of the land? Whiles it remained, was it not thine own: and after it was sold, was it not in thine own power? Why hast thou conceived this thing in thine heart? Thou hast not lied unto men, but unto God. And Ananias hearing these words fell down and gave up the ghost: and great fear came on all them that heard these things." (Acts 5:3-5(KJV)"

To know when a person is not speaking from the direction of the Holy Spirit, it would be discerned that this person is showing out in order to be recognized by their own achievements and ambitions to rise within the Body of Christ. "Beloved, believe not every spirit, but try the spirits whether they are of God: because many false prophets are gone out into the world. (1John 4:1(KJV)" It could also be determined that what they are saying **does not line up with the Word of God**. Psalms 75:5,6(KJV) says, "Lift not up your horn on high: speak not with a stiff neck. For promotion cometh neither from the east, nor from the west, nor from the south.

The Gift of Prophecy – The Apostle Paul tells the church to seek spiritual gifts, but especially that we may prophecy. When one receives Jesus as Savior and become Born Again, they receive the Holy Spirit at that time. When a person is Baptized in the Holy Spirit, this means they have been immersed in the Holy Spirit. "Follow after charity, and desire spiritual gifts, but rather that ye may prophesy." (1 Corinthians 14:1(KJV) Here the Apostle Paul explains to the Church at Corinth that the most important duty of a Christian should be to walk in love. Spiritual maturity also comes with the Word of Knowledge and Wisdom, which is not the gift of Prophecy, but the Holy Spirit imparts a level to speak from God. When one receives Jesus as Savior, the Holy Spirit comes in at that time. But when a person is Baptized in the Holy Spirit, you have been immersed in the Holy Spirit. "And it shall come to pass in the last days, saith God, I will pour out of my Spirit upon all flesh: and your sons and your daughters shall prophesy, and your young men shall see visions, and your old men shall dream dreams. (Acts 2:17(KJV)"

Prophetic Messages are Divinely spoken and would not have been humanely prepared or thought through by the speaker. Prophecy is important as at meeting times, many persons who would be attending church, or may not be seeking the Lord, could be benefitted to hear a direct word from which brings physical healing, spiritual encouragement and conviction to their lives. "But he that prophesieth speaketh unto men to edification and exhortation and comfort. He that speaketh in an unknown tongue edfieth himself, but he that prophesieth edifieth the church. (1 Corinthians 14:3-4(KJV)"

Diverse Tongues – Tongues is a Supernatural gift of speaking in different tongues that even the speaker cannot understand, as he/ she is speaking **foreign languages that God alone has given them**. They would not have previously learned it. Acts 2:4(KJV) speaks that those in the church spoke in their own native tongue at the same time, under the inspiration of the Holy Spirit. Paul reminded the church at 1 Corinthians 12:4(KJV), "Now there are diversities of gifts but the same spirit."

The Interpretation of Tongues - Interpretation of Tongues brings to understanding **what has been said when a Diverse Tongue was spoken**. The Holy Spirit causes the interpreter to speak forth what was said, which brings out the meaning of the message which was said in tongues. Interpretation of Togues should not be confused with the interpretation of languages, where a student studies Languages and then works as an Interpreter of Foreign Languages as spoken in the world. The gift of Interpretation of Tongues is given by the Holy Spirit. "If any man speak in an unknown tongue, let it be by two, or at the most by three, and that by course; and let one interpret. But if there be no interpreter, let him keep silence in the church; and let him speak to himself, and to God. (1 Corinthians 14:27-28(KJV)"

The Gift of Faith - Each one has a measure of Faith! **When we believed for Salvation through The Blood of Jesus, our salvation came through Grace by Faith.** But as one grows in Grace and maturity, and hears God's Voice more clearly, we will receive more instructions and commands from Him, e.g. if someone is hurt in a weather storm and there is no way to get medical help, the Lord will impress upon you to pray for healing. In God's Word you will find out that the words 'faith' and 'believing' can be used interchangeably, and they mean the same thing. The Holy Spirit, our Helper comes in to help us, by strengthening our courage, giving us extraordinary confidence to stand on God's Word. In Faith believing, you will know that God is with you to get done that which needs to be completed for His Kingdom through you. "Now Faith is the substance of things hoped for, the evidence of things not seen. (Hebrews 11:1(KJV)" The Holy Spirit gives us the courage to stand in faith and believe God, putting our unbelief and fearful reasoning out of the way. **Faith is to have confidence in God despite how the situation looks**. God imparts the gift of healing to Christians through the Holy Spirit. Since all Christians have different dispositions and attitudes towards certain areas of Ministry, the Holy Spirit knows which Christians would be best suited for the job of the Gift of Healing. "Insomuch that they brought forth the sick into the streets and laid them on beds and couches, that at the least the shadow of Peter passing by might overshadow some of them. There came also, a multitude out of the cities round about unto Jerusalem, bringing sick folks, and them which were vexed with unclean spirits and they were healed every one. (Acts 5:15-16(KJV)"

The Working of Miracles – God's supernatural power is used through the Holy Spirit to perform miracles that otherwise could not happen. It could be that God is sending help to one of His Children just on time. "Then the king commanded, and they brought Daniel, and cast him into the den of lions. Now the king spoke and said unto Daniel, thy God whom thou servest continually, he will deliver thee. (Daniel 6:16(KJV)" A Miracle is an extraordinary act that can only have happened by God. A human does not necessarily have to perform the miracle, but when one happens everyone knows it is from God. Another miracle from God, "And Peter answered Him and said, Lord, if it be Thou, bid me come unto thee on the water. And He said, come, and when Peter was come down out of the ship, he walked on the water, to go to Jesus. (Matthew 14:28-29(KJV)"

THE FRUIT OF
THE SPIRIT

God gave us the Fruit of the Spirit (Galatians 5:22, 23(KJV), to teach us how to live our lives from His Spirit. There are nine Spiritual fruit, love, joy, peace, longsuffering, kindness, goodness, faithfulness, meekness, temperance, which are meant to help us live a fruitful life. You would find that each of the nine fruit of the spirit, would bring good structure to life and we cannot do without these. Before Jesus came to earth and died for us, the Jews were expected to follow the Law (the Ten Commandments) and people would have interpreted the law however they felt in their heart to do. If someone made them angry, they dealt with it however they saw necessary, which meant persons could have been carelessly killed, or parts of their limbs cut off e.g. if someone was found stealing, his hand could be cut off. The Holy Spirit has brought to us the privilege to live more meaningful and purposeful lives. By understanding that, "The Joy of the Lord is your strength, spoken of at Nehemiah 8:10(KJV)." The Holy Spirit imparts the strength to stand in joy regardless to whatever is going on around us.

Before we discuss the Fruit of the Spirit further, it is important to advise you that there are also Works of the Flesh. Both the works of the Flesh and Spirit are outlined by the Apostle Paul at Galatians 5:19-23 (KJV), "Now the works of the flesh are manifest, which are these;

adultery, fornication, uncleanness, lasciviousness, idolatry, witchcraft, hatred, variance, emulations, wrath, strife, seditions, heresies, envyings, murders, drunkenness, revellings, and such like: of the which I tell you before, as I have also told you in time past, that they which do such things shall not inherit the kingdom of God." These and everything else that did not come through the Holy Spirit are brought on by the enemy. Paul warns that those who do such things shall not inherit the kingdom of God. But the fruit of the Spirit is love, joy, peace, patience (longsuffering), kindness, goodness, faithfulness, gentleness, self-control, against such there is no law.

Love – is an attribute of God and it is completely His Nature because He is Love. "Beloved let us love one another, for love is of God; and every one that loves is born of God and knows God." (1 John 4:7(KJV) Love includes many areas, affection, benevolence, strong liking, romantic or sexual implications. For this section, we wish to emphasize the love of God, and love for your neighbor. "Charity (Love) suffers long, and is kind; charity envieth not; charity vaunteth not itself, is not puffed up, Doth not behave itself, unseemly, seeketh not her own, is not easily provoked, thinketh no evil; "rejoiceth not in iniquity, but rejoiceth in the truth; Beareth all things, believeth all things, hopeth all things, endureth all things. Charity (Love) never faileth: but whether there by prophecies, they shall fail; whether there be tongues they shall cease, whether there be knowledge, it shall vanish away. (1 Corinthians 13: 4,5(KJV)"

When we obey God's commandments not only as it relates to ourselves, but love and look out for our neighbors, especially those in need of our assistance. To love others ungrudgingly not causing shame or injury, truly Blesses God. "There is no fear in love; but perfect love casts out fear: because fear has torment and not made perfect in love. (1 John 4:18(KJV)" Jesus advised at (Mark 12: 28 – 30(KJV) that our most important responsibility is to love God. "If a man says, I love God, and hates his brother, he is a liar: for he that loves not his brother whom he has seen, how can he love God whom he has not seen? (1 John 4:20(KJV)"

Joy - may best be realized through the worship of God, as only God can impart true Joy to the heart. World joy can never compare to the Joy a Christian experiences when worshipping God in spirit and in truth, as God gives the strength to overcome even when life experiences is not filled with good success. Examine the experiences of Job {The Book of Job in the Old Testament) and what he went through, reveals that there had to be something other than good success in business to keep joy within and Job believing that God was with him despite what he was experiencing. "So, the Lord blessed the latter end of Job more than his beginning; for he had fourteen thousand sheep, and six thousand camels, and a thousand she asses. He had also seven sons and three daughters. "(Job 42:12(KJV)

Satan makes it his business to plot to bring Christians down, through mistakes and temptations which can lead to sin. But hold foremost in your heart, that the Holy Spirit dwells with you and with trust in Him, by His Mercy and Grace, we can overcome. "My bretheren, count it all joy when ye fall into Divers temptations; knowing this, that the trying of your faith worketh patience." (James 1:2-3(KJV) We have got to hold on to knowing that the Holy Spirit is with us, even in times of uncertainty when you do not know what will happen next, stand strong knowing that God is there. "Be strong and of a good courage, fear not, nor be afraid of them: for the Lord thy God, He it is that doth go with thee; He will not fail thee, nor forsake thee. (Deuteronomy 31:6(KJV)"

To know and understand that God's Love is unconditional and the Holy Spirit remains with us, whether we are in a period of peace or going through a time a sorrow, our duty is to keep foremost in our mind that He is there. This should bring us joy! "Thou wilt show me the path of life: in thy presence is fullness of joy; at thy right hand there are pleasures for evermore." (Psalm 16:11(KJV) Let us be mindful that God is always there, and when we falter through mistakes, whether in our own lives or if we have hurt another, It is The Holy Spirit who continues to prod us to make it right. Joy continues to flow with confession to God, Prayer and Thanksgiving, and doing our part in the Body of Christ, the Holy Spirit will tell us what our part is to do, that pleases God. The Apostle Paul said it, "Finally my bretheren, rejoice in The Lord. To write the same things to you, to me indeed is not grievous, but for you it is safe." (Philippians 3:1(KJV)

Peace – serenity, harmony, tranquility, well-being and or security is what each person whether they are Christian or not longs for. It is a key aspect of staying on course for Christians. As God's witnesses, we should peacefully speak of His love to others, as persons are more relaxed and confident around peacefulness. The peace of God gives one the stamina to stand regardless of what is going on around them. Peace gives courage to renew the minds of everything that is unnecessary and burdensome. "And the Peace of God, which passeth all understanding, will guard your hearts and your minds in Christ Jesus." (Philippians 4:7(KJV) Whatever is the cause of our fears or worry we yearn for peace within.

As one walks in obedience to God, seeking The Holy Spirit's directives, to bring about peace to everyone, God bestows more and more of His Peace on them. "Follow peace with all men, and holiness, without which no man shall see The Lord:" (Hebrews 12:14(KJV) There are also those who secretly plan to do evil toward others yet claim that all is well. "They have healed also the hurt of the daughter of my people slightly, saying, Peace, Peace; when there is no peace." (Jeremiah 6:14) Very importantly, when Jesus was born in Bethlehem, the multitude of angels came saying, "Glory to God in the highest, and on earth peace, good will toward men." (Luke 2:14(KJV)

Jesus, The Prince of Peace came to earth for the purpose to redeem us from our sins, because the only path to lasting peace comes from The Prince of Peace. It is our duty to let the Peace of God rule in our hearts, or we trust in ourselves where our life can turn out to be a failure. Let us allow the Spirit of God to overflow us with His Divine

Peace, as being spiritually minded brings life and Peace, (Romans 8:6. (KJV) Then we can surely live His Peace before others.

Patience - in the Oxford Dictionary, is the ability to put up calmly with delay, inconvenience, or annoyance without becoming angry. Tolerance, endurance, long suffering, and forbearance are words which also describe patience. We live in a world where unexpected negative situations can quickly change the course of normalcy. So, when your patience has been tried, or you are openly mocked or taken advantage of, even by those you trusted, it is best to prayerfully pause before responding angrily in frustration. Because you are a new Creation in Christ Jesus, strength imparted by The Holy Spirit will be with you as you stand in His Glory. "But thou, O Lord, art a God full of compassion, and gracious, longsuffering, and plenteous in mercy and truth." (Psalm 86:15(KJV) The Lord will allow many ways for his people to grow in patience and after one has been tried many times, patience would be understood.

There are those who may believe patience is for the weak and passive, who run from confrontation, or allow others to mishandle or cheat them out of what God has given them. This is not true as a Christian should persevere and endure hard trials, but also depends on the Holy Spirit for direction in how to handle situations, without getting frazzled. "The Lord is slow to anger, and great in power, and will not at all acquit the wicked: the Lord hath His way in the whirlwind and in the storm, and the clouds are the dust of his feet." (Nahum 1:3(KJV)

As long as all is going well, we can be in a good place, but when we feel that someone has done us wrong or we've been dealt unfairly in a matter, then we become hurt and feel our rights have been trampled on. But the gift of the Spirit in Patience, is there to draw out maturity from within. "Let Patience have her perfect work, that ye may be perfect and entire, wanting nothing." (James 1:4(KJV) This teaches how we walk in humility, checking our attitude by not being easily angered or have temper tantrums, but remaining still, knowing that The Lord will be with you in whatever you face.

Kindness – thoughtful, gentle, helpful, benevolent, sympathetic, and courteous, all describe the word kindness. It means, to be considerate and/or polite to others, because our Father God is our first example and His kindness is given without condition. He still loves regardless to whether you have displayed good or bad behavior. "For His merciful kindness is great toward us and the truth of the Lord endures forever. Praise ye the Lord." (Psalm 117:2(KJV) One should never seek to repay wrongs done, because we know that the all-seeing Eye of God is covering us, and He will respond. "Not rendering evil for evil, or railing for railing: but contrariwise blessing; knowing that ye are thereunto called, that ye should inherit a blessing." (1 Peter 3:9(KJV)

God's love and kindness is unconditional, therefore if we are to be like Jesus, we should be kind. These are times in our world when much migration and travelling is taking place, because of unrest in many places. This is also where one's full trust must be in The Holy Spirit, in how to treat everyone, and who you should allow or not allow to get close to you, bearing in mind that you may be entertaining angels unawares. "Be not forgetful to entertain strangers: for thereby some have entertained angels unawares." (Hebrews 13:2(KJV)

Goodness - speaks about God's goodness to us, even when we have not been good to Him. This is understood as kindness. Therefore, it is His Goodness that brings us to repentance of our sins, showing us how to live for Christ. He has given His goodness to us by forgiving us, therefore we are expected to forgive others for the wrongs they have done to us, giving us an opportunity to be good to them. Jesus answered the ruler who asked, saying, "Good Master, what shall I do to inherit eternal life?" (Luke 18:18(KJV) Jesus said to him, "Why callest thou me good? None is good, save one, that is God." (Luke 18:19(KJV) The Bible says that God is Good because His attributes are good, He can only be good. To portray goodness is to live the gifts of the Spirit, which is righteous uprightness. Let us follow the example of Jesus, when He was on the earth, He went about doing good. Jesus is truly the perfect example for us. "Surely goodness and mercy shall follow me all the days of my life: (Psalm 23:6(KJV)."

Faithfulness - God is faithful toward us and it teaches us how to also be faithful by being consistently true, reliable, steadfast, and dependable, thus causing us to remain humble. The Apostle Paul wrote to the church at Colosse, "To the saints and faithful bretheren in Christ which are at Colosse: Grace be unto you, and peace, from God our Father and the Lord Jesus Christ." (Colossians 1:2(KJV) A good example of faithfulness both to God and man was Joseph, when he was propositioned by Potiphar's wife to commit adultery with her. Joseph refused to sin before God. He was then thrown in prison because she lied, saying Joseph tried to seduce her. But Joseph remained faithful and was eventually released from prison to become the greatest leader in Egypt, next to Potiphar. God rewarded him for his faithfulness. (Genesis 39:1-6(KJV)

Gentleness - is the gift that is also seen as kindness and meekness. Being gentle may seem weak, but it is really a great strength. A truly gentle person can still be polite after being crushed in spirit by something terribly mean that has happened to them. They can still stand without going into a rage of anger regardless of the situation.

When we live a peaceful and exemplary life before others, especially those persons who are younger, it is much easier to be an example. Also, they would be more open to receiving correction from us. "But the wisdom that is from above is first pure, then peaceable, gentle, and easy to be intreated, full of mercy and good fruits, without partiality and without hypocrisy. (James 3:17(KJV)"

Self-Control - or self-discipline is an area of great importance. In order to win the race that is set before us, we are to live disciplined lives before God. This is easier said than done as in this world there are so many distractions designed by the enemy to take our focus away from staying in the race. "Know ye not that they which run in a race run all, but one receives the prize? So run, that you may obtain. And every man that strives for the mastery is temperate in all things. Now they do it to obtain a corruptible crown; but we an incorruptible." (1 Corinthians 9:24-25(KJV)

Even as our help comes from the Lord, it is why He has sent the Holy Spirit to dwell within us and walk alongside us on the earth giving us the power we need to overcome through self-discipline. This is very important to Christians, as some of the areas where we can indulge ourselves are, overeating and becoming obese; overspending and purchasing things above our budget; jealousy or being envious over what someone else possesses, whether it's their spouse, home, vehicle, job or clothing etc.; gossiping and tale-baring; judging others; watching movies Christians should not watch, such as X-rated; engaging in sexual activity outside of marriage; worry and complaining. "So, then they that are in the flesh cannot please God. But ye are not in the flesh, but in the Spirit, if so be that the Spirit of God dwell in you. (Romans 8:8,9(KJV)

"There hath no temptation taken you but such as is common to man: but God is faithful, who will not suffer you to be tempted above that ye are able; but will with the temptation also make a way to escape, that ye may be able to bear it. (1 Corinthians 10:13(KJV)"

Knowing When
God Is Speaking

---❖---

God speaks continuously, but how much are we able to hear Him? As humans, we speak from person to person. But as Christians, we also speak to God and expect that He has heard us and sometimes we do not get an answer. The good thing is we are given the privilege to delight in the Lord, loving on our Father God. "Delight thyself also in the Lord; and He shall give thee the desires of thine heart (Psalm 37:4(KJV)." God is Omnipresent, Sovereign and All-Powerful. First, we should be able to understand how God Speaks and what is unique to us. Then if we do understand that He has spoken, would we be willing to accept and be obedient to do what He wishes to be done.

In the Old Testament God spoke to His people in various ways when He wished to get His message to them. We serve a creative God and some ways we can hear God Speak include, Through the Word of God; Through the Teachings of Jesus; Through the Still Small Voice of The Holy Spirit; Through Dreams, Visions; Word of Knowledge; Word of Wisdom; Through Prophecy; Via Angels; Through Circumstances; Through our Inner Convictions or Intuition and Through Other People etc. "The heavens declare the glory of God, and the firmament sheweth His handywork. Day unto day uttereth speech, and night unto night sheweth knowledge." (Psalms 19:1-2(KJV). Here are some ways believers can hear God speak to them:

Through the Teachings of Jesus – Jesus was sent to the earth by God the Father to do all that God told Him to do which was mainly giving His life to redeem us from sin. That which He did was orchestrated by God. His life depicts how He lived free from sin and overcame every act of temptation; He turned water into wine; Loved the down-trodden, placing much emphasis on the care of women and children; He did not turn away those in need of healing, e.g. Jairus' daughter (Matthew 9:18-26(KJV), the woman with the issue of blood (Matthew 9:20-22(KJV), blind Bartimaeus (Mark 10:45-52(KJV), to name a few; how He taught by example as He knew which one of His disciples would betray Him to be crucified, yet He did not treat Judas with scorn, etc. Jesus speaks to us through the Gospels, Matthew, Mark, Luke, and John. He says to us, "My sheep hear my voice and I know them, and they follow me: and I give them eternal life; and they shall never perish, neither shall any man pluck them out of my hand." (John 10:27-28(KJV) Jesus also gave us a promise that, "Verily, verily, I say unto you, He that believeth on me, the works that I do shall he do also; and greater works than these shall he do; because I go to My Father." (John 14:12(KJV) Jesus came to restore us back to God through redemption from that which Adam did when he sinned in the Garden of Eden. "Except a man be born again, he cannot see the kingdom of God, (John 3:3(KJV)."

Through the Sermon on the Mount at Matthew 5: 3-12(KJV), Jesus taught the eight powerful blessings which are known as the Beatitudes, which were given for Divine Favor to believers. You will see that, each begin with the word 'Blessed', which shows us that each of us can possess these qualities. They also give one hope for rewards both on the earth and in Heaven and points each believer to what it means to be a true disciple. Jesus also gave us the method of how to pray, "Our Father which art in Heaven, Hallowed by Thy Name thy kingdom come. Thy will be done in earth, as it is in heaven. Give us this day our daily bread. And forgive us our debts, as we forgive our debtors. And lead us not into temptation but deliver us from evil. For thine is the kingdom, and the power, and the glory, forever. Amen! (Matthew 6:9-13(KJV)." This prayer was to remind Israel that God still loved His People and His wish was that they serve the God of Heaven (God the Father, God the Son and The Holy Spirit). This prayer was also meant for the gentile Christians, which would be us, as we have been adopted as sons and daughters by God when we became believers. One of the most important aspects of the Lord's Prayer is that it points us to the need for forgiveness of each other. "For if we forgive men their trespasses, your heavenly Father will also forgive you: But if ye forgive not men their trespasses, neither will your Father forgive your trespasses (Matthew 6:14-15(KJV)."

Now before Jesus ascended into Heaven, we understand that He coached His disciples well for the job, "Verily, Verily, I say unto you, He that believeth on me, the works that I do shall he do also; and greater works than these shall he do; because I go unto my Father (John 14:12(KJV)." Therefore, the entire New Testament bears the teachings and workings of Jesus, as He prepared His disciples to carry on when He left. "And He said unto them, go ye into all the world and preach the gospel to every creature. He that believeth and is baptized shall be saved; but he that believeth not shall be damned. And these signs shall follow them that believe; In my name shall they cast out devils; they shall speak with new tongues; they shall take up serpents; and if they drink any deadly thing, it shall not hurt them; they shall lay hands on the sick and they shall recover. So then after the Lord had spoken unto them, he was received into heaven and sat on the right hand of God. And they went forth and preached everywhere, the Lord working with them and confirming the Word with signs following. Amen! (Mark 16:15-20(KJV)." One of those disciples would be the Apostle Paul, who came to Christ after Jesus ascended to Heaven and also would take his first Missionary Journey (Acts 13:1-3(KJV).

Through His Word – God speaks to us through His Word. Every time we read the Bible, we can hear God speaking within our spirit, just ask Him when we do not understand. Even as He is always speaking, He also wants to hear our questions and He answers immediately. Just trust and know that you will hear Him speak to your spirit, so listen for His Voice, because He speaks to us through our spirit. The way you train your spirit to hear from God, is to get in complete silence, not allowing the enemy to speak in your spirit, or not thinking of anything else, but His love for you, so thank Him within. Now as you know, the enemy would always seek to give you an answer also. But the enemy's answers are fabricated and never totally true because, he is a liar, and was one from the beginning. He would always twist God's Word to sound truthful to you but, remember how he twisted the Word when he spoke to Eve in the Garden of Eden, and because Eve did not know exactly what God had said to Adam, she obeyed the serpent. Listen for God's answer, which would be based on the true Word of God. You would therefore, have to know the Word, which stays with you by daily study of His Word. When you know the Word of God clearly, you will not be led by deception from the enemy, as the Holy Spirit will not tell you to take any action contrary to God's Word. "I will worship toward thy holy temple and praise thy name for thy lovingkindness and for thy truth: for thou hast magnified thy word above all thy name (Psalm 138:2(KJV)." We are to know and understand God's Word without wavering. Even as God stands on the pure truthfulness of His Word, and stamps it, we too can stand on God's Word just as if we had taken out a Contract and signed our name at the bottom and it is stamped. The stamp for us in the Word is, **IN THE NAME OF JESUS.**

Every message we get through God's Word is meant to bring Glory and Honor to His Name. We cannot add or take away from God's Word. If we do this, we would be working right in the hands of the enemy. Sometimes believers can get overly zealous in sharing the Word and unknowingly change the correct quotes, which then the meaning of that Verse changes from what it is meant to be and how it is quoted in the Bible. It is therefore truth to walk in the spirit hence not fulfilling the lust of the flesh. This can also happen when someone is giving a word of Knowledge in the Church or to an individual Christian. If one is well versed with the Word of God, it is easy to detect whether that one is speaking truth or not. It is important to know the Word of Truth which comes from God's Word, it saves one from being duped. "Sanctify them through thy truth: thy word is truth. As thou hast sent me into the world, even so have I also sent them into the world." (John 17:17(KJV)

Through Dreams and Visions - The Bible has given many accounts where God revealed His Will to His people through dreams and visions. We know that Joseph began to have dreams as a little boy, he didn't know God was preparing him to become ruler of Egypt; God spoke through the Prophet Samuel, that he was to anoint David to be king, (1 Samuel 16(KJV); Moses and the burning bush (Exodus 3:1-4(KJV); God sends an angel to Manoah's wife, giving her the news that she would give birth to a son - Samson (Judges 13(KJV); In the New Testament we see that God sent the angel Gabriel to Zacharias to tell him that his wife Elizabeth would bear a son and call his name John, (Luke 2:11-25(KJV); The angel Gabriel was sent from God to Mary and told her that she would conceive a son through the power of the Holy Ghost. She shall call His Name Jesus who would be the Savior of the world, (Luke 26-36KJV).

Dreams and Visions are a part of the supernatural experiences from God. A vision is that which is inspired by God for you to see. A dream is that which you see in your sleep. Or it can be that which you imagine in your mind pertaining to your goals in life. I believe He gives us dreams and visions because throughout the busyness of life, i.e. family, employment, other church activities etc., we do not allow Him to get our attention during our waking hours, as we may not have as much time during the daytime. Even as we may say we are not lax in seeking Him enough, it does show us that within a busy day we may not be able to listen well enough and He is always speaking.

Even so, He knows our heart and certainly our sincerity towards His Holy Spirit. It can happen to every believer! When you have a vision or a dream, always check and see if it aligns with the Word of God, because God works with His Word. Let us not forget that our minds can cause us to get carried away, and the enemy is very deceptive. Write your dream or vision down, so you can continually pray about it to reach clarification. Also, if you trust another believer who is mature in the Word, ask them to pray both with and for you regarding what you have seen in your dream or vision if it bothers you. They can also help you search the scriptures based on what you have seen. Have you not heard a family member or someone at work, or church say, I had the craziest dream last night! That means they do not understand what they saw while they slept, but they still remember it and it troubles them. The closer we get to God and understand His Word, we will begin to comprehend what we have seen as we allow His Spirit to speak of each situation. "And it shall come to pass in the last days, saith God, I will pour out of my spirit upon all flesh: and your sons and your daughters shall prophesy, and your young men shall see visions, and your old men shall dream dreams:" (Acts 2:17(KJV))

When we **Dream,** God speaks to us through Parables, that is, the meaning is not openly clear to us. Jesus spoke in parables when He ministered sometimes. "A sower went out to sow his seed: and as he sowed, some fell by the wayside; and it was trodden down, and the fowls of the air devoured it. And some fell upon a rock; and as soon as it was sprung up, it withered away, because it lacked moisture. And some fell among thorns; and the thorns sprang up with it and choked it. And other fell on good ground and sprang up and bore fruit an hundredfold and when he had said these things, he cried, He that hath ears to hear let Him hear (Luke 8: 5-15(KJV)." Jesus revealed the meaning of where each seed fell, thus giving reasons why some of the seeds did not grow because of the kind of ground they fell on (Luke 8:11-14(KJV) and why those that fell on good ground grew (verse 15). Likewise, when we have a dream, the real meaning may be hidden to us at first. I do not know why God would do it this way, but He knows how to get our attention, He alone is God, we should therefore trust Him to reveal the answer to us.

Now here is a dream you may have dreamt already! Have you ever dreamt you were running, and it is continuous, you have the same dream recurring over and over many nights? This is because the Holy Spirit can prompt your spirit through intuition, and you know you are moving in the spirit, you are not stagnant. Which means you are growing stronger spiritually toward your purpose. Therefore, just trust Him, to guide you to where He wants you to be and remain faithful to Him. Now the place where God wants you to be can either be toward the Ministry Giftings that He has given you, or it can be either professional or educational standing in your life. To be stagnant is to remain standing in the same place, not moving. Spiritually not moving forward in their life experience. When water is stagnant this means, it is not flowing, is still and becomes stale, according to the Oxford Dictionary. To dream of running is a good dream.

Also know that you may have reoccurring dreams. God may be giving you a warning that something is going to happen. It may be about a family member, a friend, persons you do not personally know, or your country. God gives these types of dreams to those whom He trusts to pray for others. This is when you need to pray for the well-being and progress of those you have seen in the dream and for their eminent Salvation if they are not yet Christians. Sometimes dreams like this may reoccur until it happens in real life, so keep interceding. You know the Lord was prompting you in dreams when what you have dreamt while asleep, comes to pass in real life. Do not use dream books, these do not line up with the Word of God. Trust the Holy Spirit!

Through **Visions** one is seeing literally what will come to pass. Most visions occur during one's conscious waking hours. Daniel saw the Ancient of Days sitting on His Throne (Daniel 7:9-10(KJV); God told

Abraham he was to have a biological son, and his generations would be as the stars in number, (Genesis 15: 1-5(KJV); Peter, James and John saw the Vision of Jesus' Transfiguration into Heaven (Matthew 17:1-9(KJV); The total Book of Revelation was seen by the Apostle John (Revelation Chapters 1-22(KJV).

The Lord gave me a Vision some years ago, where He spoke into my spirit to pray for those whom He showed to me. There was to be a Ministry meeting of which I was to be a participant. I awoke early as always to pray and even as I lay there, suddenly I saw before my eyes some of the persons who were also scheduled to participate in the same meeting. These persons were speaking degrading things about prospective attendees. It was as if I was no longer in bed but standing right where they were, as I clearly heard their words, saw their clothing and where they were standing during their conversation. This vision could not have been more than a minute. Suddenly I sat up in bed astonished, not knowing whether I had fallen asleep again. On arriving to the meeting later that day, my heart fell, as each of those persons were wearing the exact same clothing that I had seen them wearing in the vision. I knew my job was to pray for them and not discuss with others.

When God trusts us with a matter, I believe He does not mean that we act on it by discussing with others. We should be trusted to pray for those involved in wrongful acts. It would mean people changing the way they believe and turn their lives completely over to Jesus. That's why I believe He told me to intercede, as those persons are also His children and He is a good Father who wants His children to remain focused in completing their assignment in the earth. When God gives the intuition to pray for anyone, we cannot take it lightly as He sees the end from the beginning of every situation. Those persons seemed to grow stronger in their stand for Him over the years and it was a privilege to pray. Visions are Supernatural and cover many areas usually foretelling the future. These can reveal the truth of a matter, thus directing each to the Will of God, giving hope, encouragement, and Purpose for His People. An important point Christians must always bear in mind is that we should be obedient to God when He prompts us to do a thing.

Via Angels – God sends Angels to bring messages to mankind. The name Angel means Messenger. Their duty is to bring messages to the heirs of salvation, which are vital for hope, protection, comfort, service to others, Judgement and Praise to God.

"And entering in to the sepulchre, they saw a young man sitting on the right side clothed in a long white garment, and they were affrighted. And he saith unto them, be not affrighted: Ye seek Jesus of Nazareth, which was crucified: he is risen; He is not here: behold the place where they laid him. But go your way, tell His disciples and Peter that He goeth before you into Galilee: there shall ye see Him, as He said unto you (Mark 16:5-7(KJV)."

"And I saw another Angel fly, in the midst of heaven, having the everlasting gospel to preach unto them that dwell on the earth, and to every nation, and kindred, and tongue, and people. Saying with a loud voice, Fear God, and give glory to Him for the hour of His Judgement is come: and worship Him that made Heaven, and earth, and the sea, and the fountains of waters (Revelation 14:6-7(KJV)."

About thirty-eight years ago, as a young mother experiencing life's difficulties and raising my young children, I learned quickly how to depend on Prayer and pressing into the Holy Spirit's presence to get me through the day-to-day stresses. I would pray with my family earlier each night then when I awoke later during the night or early morning, I would get up and pray in the living-room area of our home. One night after praying, I believe it had to be around 2:00 a.m. I returned to my room, to get back into bed and there standing at the foot of my bed, was an Angel. I do not remember being fearful, because there was an awesome peace that came over me at that moment. What I witnessed was the pure whiteness of His Robe and the love in his eyes. He did not smile or open His mouth to speak, neither did He seem angry with me. Then I understood within my spirit what He was saying to me, 'I am always with you!', I heard within my spirit. There was a kind and comforting glow on His face. His brown eyes were peacefully looking straight into my face and my eyes. I just felt the peace that was emanating from His presence. I saw Him plainly even though the light on my nightstand was off. The whole incident must have transpired for only a few seconds. I became very weak and my head rested on the pillow and I must have fallen asleep. When I awoke again it had begun to get light outside, my strength had returned to me and I was fine, but I knew that God was with me, and I remembered that I saw an Angel right there in my room a few hours earlier. I told a friend whom I trusted, who obviously would have told others that I said I had seen an Angel and this news spread somewhat. I even encountered a backlash or two from some Christians, in which they tried to make me believe I had made it up and it did not happen, because others in the Body of Christ, those who had titles up the Ministerial ladder, had not seen an Angel so why would God send an Angel to visit me. I therefore said nothing else about it, but this open-eyed encounter has never left me although I did not talk about it anymore. This encounter gave me the confidence I needed to press through. Years later, I asked the Lord in prayer, "Father why didn't the Angel I saw have wings?" He answered instantly within my spirit, "Because I Came!"

Through Prayer - Although most people may not have ever heard God speak audibly, we can hear Him speak through our spirit or intuition. This is when we make time to meet with God and even after we have made our requests to Him, it is when we remain quiet and still so that we will hear from Him. "But let patience have her perfect work, that ye may be perfect and entire, wanting nothing (James 1:4(KJV)." So even after we have had our quiet time with God and have interceded for our family and others, we should remain in expectation, as God may not necessarily speak during our quiet time. This is how God perfects our patience in Him, He is God and will not allow anyone to put Him on a roster or schedule. Also, God is Holy and not likened to our secular business persons, whom we might confront when we do not get a response from a query which we may have. "Likewise, the Spirit also helpeth our infirmities: for we know not what we should pray for as we ought: but the Spirit itself makes intercession for us with groanings which cannot be uttered. And he that searcheth the hearts and knoweth, what is the mind of the Spirit, because He maketh intercession for the saints according to the will of God (Romans 8:26, 27(KJV)." We do not know how or what to pray for, but the Holy Spirit helps us in our weaknesses and intercedes for us when we need Him. During these times, it is beneficial to pray in our prayer language. When we pray in tongues, the Holy Spirit is praying within our spirit and knows exactly what we should be saying to God, which helps us get a sure answer. "For there is one God and one mediator between God and man, the man Christ Jesus; (1 Timothy 2:5(KJV)"

Through His Still Small Voice, The Holy Spirit seeks to keep us on course, nudging us when we are wrong. He encourages, disciplines, directs, dwells within, and convicts us. "Even the Spirit of Truth, whom the world cannot receive, because it seeth Him not, neither knoweth Him: but ye know Him; for He dwelleth with you and shall be in you (John 14:17(KJV)." The world is carnal, they are unable to understand the Holy Spirit or bear witness to His presence. But we know the Holy Spirit, He is our Comforter and Guide. It is He who stands with us in every situation, even when we make missteps in our walk before God, He walks alongside us, keeping us from danger. Even though he would chide us, many times through our spirit (speaking to us) letting us know when we grieve, or please The Lord. He also guides us in making daily decisions and we know when a decision is correct when our pride or ego is not getting the better of us and we are not making decisions just to look good before others. Also, many times in our busy schedules we leave God out and spend less and less time with Him. We have all done silly things that did not turn out well for us and we acted too swiftly and ended up suffering the consequences of our mistakes. "Howbeit when He, the Spirit of Truth is come, He will guide you into all truth: for He shall not speak of Himself, but whatsoever He shall hear, that shall He Speak: and He will show you things to come." (John 16:13(KJV) He speaks to us in a still small voice within our spirit.

Sometimes when I get so busy, even though I have a special time to meet with God each day, I still hear Him say within my spirit that I should come to Him in prayer, now. I obey right away, He may not have called the name of a friend or family member to me, but I know it is for an important reason and usually when I begin to Pray, He would direct me what or whom to pray for. God also speaks to you through **intuition** which is through your feelings and that still small voice. At times He may say, go and tell that person about Jesus, or pray with that one. He may even tell you which area to serve in at your Church. Let us trust knowing that when we ask Him, He will speak to us in His still small voice.

God Speaks, even in His Silence. At John 11(KJV), Jesus did not answer the call to go to Lazarus's house immediately, even though he knew, Lazarus who had been sick for two days had now died. Jesus could have answered the call when He received the message as soon as he heard it. He could have also spoken the Word that his friend be healed from the illness from wherever He was, as distance would not have made a difference with Jesus. Shortly after Lazarus had now died, Jesus decides to go to Bethany and now Lazarus had been dead for two days and was buried. Jesus might have allowed this to happen for purpose, so that the disciples' faith could be strengthened. Notice at John 14:12(KJV) He tells His disciples, "Verily, Verily, I say unto you, He that believeth on me, the works that I do shall He do also, and greater works than these shall ye do; because I go unto my Father." I believe this Word is for us today as well, as Jesus was Teacher for the disciples, and us. God wants to strengthen our faith, so that we can do the greater work on the earth in bringing others to Him, through witnessing and inviting others to Salvation, praying healing for the sick and being living examples in Jesus' Name.

Word of Knowledge, Word of Wisdom – A Word of **Knowledge** spoken to you should confirm that which you know God has already said within your heart, now coming through A Spirit of Discernment given by God. If someone gives a Word of Knowledge which does not connect with your spirit and life, it could be that one is speaking from his/her own mind, or even listening to something the enemy has said to them about a matter. Always stay close to the Lord and allow Him to guide your spirit. This would help by keeping a clean heart towards others. One should never want to be known as a gossiper, then saying they discerned a thing when it is only justifying and judging someone within their own mind. God is not a trouble-maker, He is pure! When we form negative opinions about others, this is sin and does not come from the Holy Spirit. If the person bringing a Word of Knowledge has The Holy Spirit within and the one, they are giving the message to also has The Holy Spirit, then they would know whether the word given is from God or not. Also, to give a Word Of knowledge to one who is not strong spiritually can also cause havoc and negativism. "Be not deceived; God is not mocked: for whatsoever a man soweth, that shall he also reap (Galatians 6:7(KJV)." When we sow good seed, we reap that which is good; the flesh only reaps corruption.

A Word of **Wisdom** would be spoken to you about something that will happen for you in the future also giving you a Word to know what to do at the time you may need to act on a situation. True Words of Wisdom would always resonate within a hearer. Words of Wisdom are sent by God to edify, to build up, lift-up, correct and encourage while also corresponding with His written Word. The evil forces by the enemy keeps a close track of you because He does not know what God is planning to do in your life for the future. Any inkling of something good, he seeks to give you a hard time to either keep it from happening or at least delay it. By example, Your Department Head has given you a report he wishes to have completed and handed to him an hour prior to an important meeting with Executives. That may be a time when you find it difficult to complete this easy task because of the many interruptions you have been experiencing throughout the course of the work-day. Do you really believe that the stress you were under during those few hours were normal, or was it from the enemy? Because the enemy watches you, he knows what is important to you and could try to work against you in the event you are being observed for future promotion, and would seek to make it appear you are unable to perform well under pressure.

The Lord is on your side in difficult situations and is also watching your performance, and with trust you will get the best as you stand for Him. "But the manifestation of the Spirit is given to every man to profit withal. For to one is given by the Spirit the Word of Wisdom: to another the Word of Knowledge by the same Spirit; (1 Corinthians 12:7-8(KJV)." Should someone give you a Word of Wisdom or Word of Knowledge, always test the spirit to see that it lines up with the Word of God and, by intuition within your own spirit. You would know whether that word is from God! Sometimes believers who claim to have been given the gift of Word of Knowledge, can also get caught up in gossip, or tale baring, then seek to give Words of Knowledge or Wisdom based on what is in their natural mind. If this should happen to you, put it in the Lord's hand and He would surely lift you up and bring you forward standing strong in Him in due course.

Hearing God Through Prophecy – A Prophet is a calling from God. A true Prophet should know whether God has called them to be a Prophet. "And He gave some, Apostles; and some, Prophets: and some, Evangelists; and some, Pastors and Teachers. For the perfecting of the saints, for the work of the ministry, for the edifying of the body of Christ: (Ephesians 4:11-12(KJV)." God uses Prophets in the church for making situations more perfect, i.e. bringing the believers in the ministry in living and walking more correctly before Him. The edifying would be the encouragement of all in the church as they seek to live by The Word. The Prophet builds up, comforts, and encourages various worshippers as the Lord would lead them. Anyone can operate in the Gift of Prophecy and they should be genuine, we are to trust God to confirm this truth to us. Prophets operating in the Gift of Prophecy have also been called to reveal God's Purposes for the Church. They also foretell what will happen within a country or region and any eminent dangers or successes to that place and the residents in the future. The Bible reveals that false Prophets will creep into the Church, we can find out who they are based on their character, which should line up with the Word, which is especially important. Every Prophecy should be based on God's Word as God does not go against His Word. "Beware of false prophets, which come to you in sheep's clothing, but inwardly they are ravenous wolves. (Matthew 7:15(KJV)."

Hearing God's Voice Through Others – God uses others to speak to us, when it seems He is unable to get our attention. At 1 Samuel 3:1-15(KJV) God gave the child Samuel a Word concerning Eli, the Priest, outlining to Samuel that He would destroy Eli's household and no sacrifice that Eli could give would suffice, because Eli did not rein in the wicked behavior of his sons. Eli knew that God must have said something to Samuel concerning him, as Samuel failed to tell him. He therefore, made Samuel say to him what God had said He was going to do. Eli knew he had done wrong in raising his sons and he accepted what God had said.

You may get a word from a total stranger, God might have, or have not sent them to you, but the words that they speak to you would resonate within you because it is a direct word, just for you which you needed.

Your spouse may say or do something for you at the right time, and you did not have to ask them to do what you needed to be done – this is the Lord. Family members including Elderly Parents or Children even those who are very young children have brought answers to prayer in their usually clear and honest way, and sometimes what they would innocently say, can save the day. At work, you may have been praying about seeking a transfer to another Department, and a colleague just haphazardly speaks about downsizing or vacancies they have heard will be taking place in other areas within the Company. Immediately you would know that you have your answer to prayer without even telling them what you were praying about.

The Holy Spirit also speaks to us through **our own consciences**. God gave each of us a conscience, which causes each of us to determine whether something is wright or wrong. That is why if you are saved with the evidence of the Holy Spirit, your conscience is pricked, and you feel guilty or ashamed, if you say or do anything that is wrong. You feel guilty if you do not do what is right towards others, when you know the Holy Spirit has impressed upon you to do right by that person. "Let us draw near with a true heart in full assurance of faith, having our hearts sprinkled from an evil conscience, and our bodies washed with pure water (Hebrews 10:22(KJV)."

A word may come to you through **Spiritual Poetry and/or Music** through Songs that have been written by others. When you read something that another person has written, or you listen to the words of a song, you receive an encouraging word from God.

The Pastor's words in his/her weekly Message brings conviction where the unsaved can receive Christ as Savior; there may also be words of correction that touch the inner spirits of Worshippers to keep them on the right course; every week many discouraged persons attend church looking for a word of encouragement to take them through the coming week, hence the Pastor's message of hope. The Pastor also gives words of challenge which prompts one to be a Christ witness. The Word comes to remind us of God's promises and what He expects that we keep as priorities in life. "But the wisdom that is from above is first pure, then peaceable, gentle, and easy to be intreated, full of mercy and good fruits, without partiality, and without hypocrisy." (James 3:17(KJV)

There are Christians who would have given their heart to the Lord for many years and are truly believers but have never done very much to become more mature in their walk before Him and it's because they are not aware that they should do so. Therefore, they are still baby Christians attending church regularly every Sunday. One does not suddenly jump from this position to begin hearing God's Voice speaking to them. What is genuinely put in one's relationship with God would be the results one can expect to achieve, as God gives each of us complete freedom to choose Him. Growth in Christ with positive results comes with a greater study of God's Word along with meditation of the scriptures and talking to God, keeping a close relationship with Him, listening for His Still Small Voice speaking into the spirit. At first The Holy Spirit will begin to reassure you, and you will indeed feel His presence with you. This would give you the peace and confidence you need to obey what He is telling you to do. It will be that He wants you to encourage another person or help them in some way. When He does, if you are not sure you understand discuss what you believe God has said into your spirit with a mature Christian whom you know not to be a gossiper, so as not to be led off course. God will always try your honesty, even though He knows what you will do. You will not move beyond the level where you are unprepared to be obedient to God. Obedience shows our Honor of Him.

It is also beneficial to understand how to be a witness for The Lord. God has called everyone to be a witness, which is our first duty as a Christian. Therefore, we can also be witnesses within the church building, either by, Intercessory Prayers, Teaching Sunday School classes, Bible study, small group teaching, alter worker, counsellor, or in the music department etc. To let someone else know of the love of Jesus. When I received Jesus into my heart and became a Born-again Christian, this kind of Ministry was mandatory at St. Peter's Baptist Evangelistic Church, where I worshipped at the time. Our Pastor, Rev. Eugene Butler made sure every worshipper was trained in this area, and we took to the streets every Saturday or Sunday afternoon in the neighborhood where the church was located to tell people about Jesus.

Sometimes we went on Street Services or outdoor services where there was one service for everyone in the neighborhood, or we went to other areas. There was also the Nassau Crusade held by the Billy Graham Evangelistic Crusade Association held from April 9 to 23 in 1967, where Dr. John Wesley White was the Speaker. My Pastor was involved in this, and our church got to be a part of the counselling team or the choir. This encouraged me to become involved in other areas where Counselling was conducted like the Bahamas Baptist yearly Crusades during the 1990's and a Member of the Girls Industrial School in the early 2000's. Also, other Community work including Ministering to the residents at the Aids Camp from 2009 to present.

God has also called some as full-time Missionaries to other countries as well. But one does not have to be in full-time Ministry to make a difference. I was blessed to work in the Public Service in my country, while still being obedient to what the Lord wanted me to do. Most of my Missions were done on the weekends, public holidays, and vacations, even as I was mom to my two children. When one has a heart to work, God will open doors for you to do so. Throughout the course of my Christian experience, God has given me the privilege to work in many areas of His Vineyard, and I am grateful to Him. This is to encourage you to also become a part in being a witness for the Lord. There is much work to be done, and if you are a born-again Christian, it is a part of why you have been called, which is to tell others about the love of Jesus Christ, whatever your station in life. You may not be one to talk very much to crowds, but your gifting from God could be singing, theatrics, sports or any other gifting God has given you. Whatever you do in life, be the best witness for Him that you can be. This is the Mandate you came to earth to complete.

TESTIMONIES ON HEARING GOD PERSONALLY

———◆◆———

I have had the opportunity to travel and do many Missions throughout the islands of the Bahamas. Some of those Missions I would have accompanied others, but most were times when I was sent by The Lord. Usually when I am to go on a mission, The Lord would give me a dream about the place, or while I am in prayer, sitting or lying before Him, I would hear His still small voice giving me the name of the place I should visit. He may have another person or have something happen to confirm what He has already made known to me. I have had the privilege to pray with many, many persons and hundreds have received Jesus Christ as Savior over the years.

Each mission has been a different experience and I have been blessed just as those I have been sent to have been blessed as well and God's Hand at work always evident. The Bahama Islands consists of a group of 700 Islands and Cays each one surrounded by water and thirty of which are inhabited. My home is in New Providence, the Capital. We call those islands we travel to from Nassau, Family Islands. To get to each place one would have to travel by boat or airplane. To date I have had the privilege to Mission on almost every inhabited island which are about thirty, some at least two or three times. Now when God sends one on a Mission, He does not reveal the whole story explaining what would happen from start to finish. He may reveal just enough information to let you know that He has spoken and as you go each step would be brought to light. This is to cause each Missionary to trust Him completely, as one walks by Faith.

Some Missions that stand out for me over the years:

The first time I was individually assigned to a mission by the Lord, was to the Family Island of Eleuthera, to Savannah Sound where I grew up. I had previously done other missions along with persons from the St. Peter's Baptist Evangelistic Church where I attended. The residents were glad to see me come. I stood on the hill in front of the old house in which I grew up with my grandparents and preached. Two of my distant cousins went with me and intently listened to my message. but it seemed no one gave their heart to the Lord at the time I was there. They then went with me to each house in the Settlement, and I prayed with many other residents.

The people in this settlement were mostly Methodist and Episcopalian and even as it seemed persons did not accept Jesus as Savior at the time I was there, I learnt later that some had indeed received Jesus as Savior. This was encouraging to me as a representative of Jesus Christ. This was in my early years of going on Missions. Many of these people were distant cousins and knew me since I was a baby girl and were much older than me. I believe God wanted me to be a witness to them for Him, I was about nineteen years old at this time. I have also been sent to Eleuthera at other times and to other Settlements, and in each place many persons have also accepted Jesus Christ as Savior.

The Lord sent me to the Island of Abaco at another time and some persons agreed to accompany me. We arrived on Friday evening at Marsh Harbor, as I was certain the Lord had spoken to my spirit that I Minister in that place. My understanding was to go into the area on the Saturday morning and talk to the people as the Lord would direct.

One person in the group was skeptical and began to comment, if the Lord had really sent you, He would have sent you to one of the other Settlements and not to the one you're speaking of, because that place is the main Settlement for the Island. There are only a few residents, businesses, and those homes where wealthy people live, and they would never open their gates for you. I became fearful and got very little sleep that night but prayed and prayed. In the morning I went with a heavy heart, wondering if I had heard correctly from the Lord. We knocked on some doors, but very few people were at home. As we drove, I kept asking the Lord within my spirit which way should I go, while I kept telling Him inwardly, 'Lord, I know you sent me here'. The same person in our group began to say, see I told you so, I know this island and the layout. Then the still small voice of the Lord said, turn the other way, when I said that, the person asked if I was sure as that was where the wealthy people lived. But within a few minutes into driving the new way we came to the beach. There were dozens of vehicles, as there were hundreds of people on the beach. I then realized that the Lord had sent me to minister at a school function. There were students, parents, teachers, Gospel Ministers, taxi drivers, food vendors and people from all walks of life etc. We ministered for hours and many persons came to the Lord through Salvation. I was also able to minister in another Settlement, Treasure Cay on this island. Also, on the Sunday morning we visited a Church and I was able to be a witness to the congregants. Because the Lord had this mission already planned and He knew what the outcome would be like. This mission was successful!

There was also another mission I was sent on by the Lord to Smith's Bay, Cat Island and that case seemed almost similar, where most people were not at home, but the Lord told me in my spirit to tell the driver to turn around and go the other way, we met many people at the all-age school, which was near the sea. After I told the people in the settlement my reason for coming from Nassau to tell them of His Love, they wanted us to go inside the school and talk to the people. I told them it was fine that we minister outside, which we did and as we began to witness to the people about the love of God. Persons began giving their heart to the Lord. There was also an elderly lady who told me she was 87 years old at the time. When I spoke to her, she began to cry, she said all these years, I have never said yes to Jesus, you are a child to me. She looked on me as a child even though I was already married. She gave her heart to the Lord that morning. When she accepted Jesus as Savior, her friends and relatives rejoiced. They said that persons came from Nassau to their settlement with the gospel, many times but this was her first time to respond by accepting Jesus into her heart.

There is an area called the Bain Town Constituency in Nassau, persons from the church where I attended at the time were carrying out missions in that area for a few Saturday afternoons. One Saturday, as we were going from house to house, the group I was with we came upon a lady sitting on her porch along with others watching us, as we were the visitors in the neighborhood. When we got to her house, one person in the group began to introduce Jesus to all those on the porch, but I felt that I needed to speak directly with the elderly lady. She immediately responded. With tears running down her cheeks she admitted she had never given her heart to the Lord. On that afternoon she accepted Jesus into her heart. She was 79 years old.

Then there was the time when I awoke around 5:30a.m. after dreaming that the Lord wanted me to go to an area near the Saint Cecilia's Catholic Church and School. In the dream I saw the wooden house, painted green with white trim, and I heard the Lord say in my spirit, stand there and tell them, "I am coming back soon and only those who are ready will go with me. Say, "Now is the time, accept the Lord while you have the chance." I got up and quickly got dressed and left home to find the place. It was not quite daylight yet, and as I still lived at home, that did not go over too well with my mother, but I still went. I knew this place was a far distance from where I lived, so I began to walk more speedily as I believed the Lord wanted me to go right away.

Thank God this was also a long time ago, and the Lord protected me because it is not safe to walk on the streets that early in the morning anymore. When I arrived at the area, I looked for the house that was painted the color I saw in my dream. There it was, I stood on the side of the street in front of that house and began to preach what the Lord had told me to say in the dream and everything else He placed in my spirit while I stood there. My little preaching message was over in about five minutes or less, I had said all I knew about preaching. I did not believe that anyone had heard me as it was still early. The next day, while on the bus, a lady was telling someone, that a girl came to that street and preached in front of the green house and the man died inside that very house at 3:00p.m. on the same day. This was a shock to me, but I was too afraid to say anything. I prayed that the man who died at this house had given his heart to receive Jesus as Savior before he passed away. You have been chosen by God from the foundation of the earth and never forget it, so be encouraged. God has chosen you, so be the witness He sent you to the earth to be.

In the early 2000's I held a week of services at a small Church in the Pear Dale area in Nassau. These services were for the school children and young persons as it was during the Summer vacation time, where I was able to give out school supplies to the students. These services were rewarding to my spirit and many received Jesus Christ as Personal Savior. I have also had the privilege to Minister in this manner a number of times both in Nassau and some Family Islands.

The above are just a few of the many times, The Lord has sent me on Missions. Always be sure that it is His Spirit you are hearing speaking into your spirit, and He will be with you every time. But this is one of the ways He used me. There are so many other ways, He may use you, so always remain open to His Spirit.

Set Apart

POEM BY MYRA COOPER

The Lord Has Indeed Set Me Apart,
And made me a part of His Remnant,
To do that which He's placed in my Heart,
Bringing Others to Know Him is My Intent!
This is the work for which I was sent.

Each Time I feel that I'm Undone,
His Love Helps me to Overcome.
Because He Is Truly the Only One,
I must surely learn to lean upon,
As with Him the Victory is always Won.

Now when I cannot explain what I've done,
Or why things have become such a mess.
In Him I'm able to deal with the stress,
As Prayer will ease every distress,
When upon His Word I can Truly Rest.

For Good Success I Will Seek to live Holy,
When There is hurt, His Hope I'll rest upon,
Trusting Him, Healing Will Quickly Begin,
As I remain true and stay in His Presence,
His Grace Increases Imparting true Essence.

By: Myra A. Cooper, 2017

Keys To Understanding How To Live A Successful Life

―――◆◆◆―――

Now that we know God does speak to His children, one should now have a clearer understanding of some of the ways God uses to communicate and how we hear His Voice through His Spirit and His Word. Also, we learnt that The Holy Spirit is God Himself, and we know that God is Love. "He that loveth not does not know God; for God is love." (1 John 4:8(KJV) Therefore the full purpose of love is that one first loves God, who shows us how to love others as well as ourselves.

Knowing that God is Love should give us inward strength and help us cope with hard situations when we are feeling weak and discouraged in spirit. We know that we can make it because The Holy Spirit is there to help us and promises to never turn His back on us. God put in us a desire and a will to change when we accepted Him into our heart. Change is never instant as we carry baggage and hidden skeletons from our past lives, especially those who came to Christ much later in life. But as we grow spiritually through the Word, we understand how to seek deliverance from our past. Although our spirit was cleansed, our body remains in the flesh and the enemy is aware of this.

Satan's attacks are subtle, and through his influence, the skeletons in one's closet can very easily pop up when one least expects, because they may not have really died. A good example of this can be if someone always used obscene language freely before they came to Salvation (Born Again). If they become aggravated sufficiently with another person, a cuss word can come flying from the lips, then they are embarrassed. I have witnessed this happen to someone before, and it was very embarrassing for that one. You see, your spirit received Christ as Savior, not your body. Therefore, the body still craves its old life and may easily act out, and if you are not listening to the Holy Spirit before you speak, then you're not even thinking about what it is doing until the act is over. Observe what happens when one is fasting and praying before God. That one may walk in the kitchen where a meal is being prepared for the family, and the aroma of the food takes them completely off track, and they find themselves eating some food when they should have been fasting. But fasting is to help us, not God. Therefore, the enemy knows that when we are fasting, we are pressing to draw closer to God, and fasting would open our eyes even more to his vices.

Pray about everything – Prayer changes things! (James 5:16(KJV) shows us how prayer changes us. This is important, as It can surely change us for the better. As we pray, we begin to see our situation differently. Because whatever our worry was, the Holy Spirit steps in and shows us a better way to deal with it, or He shows us where we went wrong on an issue, or just brings peace to the spirit. Prayer cannot change God, who is Sovereign and knows the end and final outcome of every situation. "Declaring the end from the beginning, and from ancient times the things that are not yet done, saying, My counsel shall stand, and I will do all my pleasure:" (Isaiah 46:10(KJV) Let us trust The Holy Spirit to help us in our weaknesses by revealing those things we need to work on in our lives. This means that one is to prayerfully stay on course. It helps to ensure that we are not mindlessly caught up incorrectly. It may also be best to confide in the counsel of a seasoned Christian, whom you trust to pray with you and hold you accountable concerning hard situations you might be dealing with.

Hidden skeletons can be anything from meddling in drugs; sexual sins (i.e. engaging in sex outside of marriage, or alternative life styles), mental illness (sometimes family members never seek medical help for that person and so the condition is hidden), theft (including petty theft or robbery), alcohol abuse, gossip, vulgar conversations, and the list can go on. To say one does not have the urge to indulge in where they came from would be an untruth. The Holy Spirit is there to help one begin the process of overcoming and facing personal issues. Previous sins cannot be hidden in the closet of the soul as one is in pretense of these faults if you do not confront them. Should this happen, one can easily bring on other issues into their life which could surely affect them in other ways, such as fear, pride, depression and or loneliness.

The following prayer will help you in your quest to press forward in your Christian walk. When you pray like this, it will be helpful to name those former actions that seem to stick with you, or that you may have difficulty in combatting:

> Dear Lord, I thank you for cleansing me from sin and saving my soul, I realize that the lingering sin of..... (name the sin(s) is still nagging within my soul. Father I renounce these ungodly acts from my life and spirit. I forgive.... (name the person(s) if there are others involved, or you may have to forgive yourself) and thank you for delivering me. Thank you, Father God for giving me the courage to stand strong. Help me to be a living witness to others, for you in this earth. AMEN!

This type of prayer should not only be prayed once, you can pray like this as many times as you need to, because at first you may not feel any change, but eventually you will notice the change and turnaround for better in your life. **A fervent Prayer life is most important!** Each day should begin and end with prayer. But a good tip is to remain prayerful throughout the day, as it helps to keep your mind in the right place. It is also most important to pray each day in your prayer language, which also helps one to grow in Grace and Sanctification.

Now be encouraged and continue to stand for Him. "I can do all things through Christ, which strengtheneth me." (Philippians 4:13(KJV) It is your duty to be a Witness in making His Name known in the earth, that what He did for you He will do for them. It means that He trusts you to tell others that He loves them and wants them to be ready for Heaven. It makes you a Witness for God while also adding strength to your Christian life. So, begin today, The Holy Spirit being your Helper, we trust Him to lead us and guide us into all truth. It is God's Purpose that you be on earth for such a time as this, so stay on the right course.

Even as we are admonished to help others through their hardships, many can tell stories about a broken heart and spirit. Some may have even been broken hearted while still loving someone then also having had to walk away broken and hurting. We all know of someone who has been seriously hurt. So, we have put limits on how far we are willing to go with anyone, even a spouse. We may even say to ourselves, "careful now, protect your heart." You may have carried deep wounds for many years, but God knows your disillusionment. He has promised to be with us when we are downcast, which means even as you may not be physically ill where it is outwardly seen, The Holy Spirit stands waiting to bring healing to your heart's cry, so you're not alone, even when you believe you do not feel Him near. The enemy continues to point out the insensitivity of others and what they have done to cause pain on you. It's his desire that you continue talking about your hurt. God wants you to let it go and that you press into His Love and healing will begin through His Holy Spirit. This is where the act of forgiveness is important, which also helps with your healing process. "For as the sufferings of Christ abound in us, so our consolation also, aboundeth by Christ." (2 Corinthians 10:5(KJV)

There may not be any other person who has stood with you or are even aware of what you've been going through, but know today, God loves you! Now you physically say it, **GOD LOVES ME!** You can say it over and over, and over again. God loves you, and He will never, ever leave or turn His back on you. "So that we may boldly say, The Lord is my helper, and I will not fear what man shall do unto me." (Hebrews 13:6(KJV) Now give every hurt over to The Holy Spirit, and after you do, the enemy will still try to bring it before you, but every time he does, just say thank you Jesus, I am healed.

Let's pray:

> Father I thank you for healing me of the hurt which I have endured for so long. I now realize that my part is to forgive those who have hurt me. So, I totally forgive everyone who has done me wrong, and help me to be aware how not to dwell on the hurt by thinking or speaking about it anymore. I give it all to you Lord! AMEN!

Do not just pray in this manner once, pray like this every time you need to.

Forgiving Others – Should a Christian refuse to forgive for any reason, the scenario of what happened to them remains in the soul. "If it be possible, as much as is in you, live peaceably with all men. (Romans 12:18(KJV)" Press past holding grudges and be sure to forgive, so that the hurt encountered may begin the process of healing within. You may have to do it within your own spirit many times before you begin to experience peace about it. "Jesus saith unto him (Peter), I say not unto thee, until seven times: but, until seventy times seven." (Matthew 18:22(KJV) when you forgive the person who hurt you it also frees you, not the person who did the misdeed to you. Many times, they would have forgotten it very quickly, and could care less that you are worried or hurt, they have already moved on. God's Word does not specify that you should allow that one whom you have forgiven back into your space and friendship again, as they have been found to be untrustworthy. This does not mean that you are angry with them. Trust that The Holy Spirit will reveal those whom you should allow as close friends. The fact that He's told us to forgive means that when we forgive sincerely, He will do the work within us to bring healing. God knows each heart, and He will bring their wrong deeds to each conscience as only He can. As well as cause that one to change and show responsibility for their actions if your relationship is valued by them. This can happen, even if it is a difficult spouse, continue to pray for them even after forgiving. Please bear in mind that when we do not forgive, we ourselves can become bitter.

To hold grudges or anger can contribute to other illnesses within your own body, like anxiety, depression and worry. Research has found that nursing anger and holding on to unforgiveness is a cause for serious illness developing in a person's body. Do not allow the enemy to tell you that it is not fair to you, that they would get to go free because of the awful thing they did to you. "And when ye stand praying, forgive, if ye have ought against any: that your Father also which is in heaven may forgive you your trespasses. (Mark 11:25(KJV)" Let's remember, when we realize we have sinned and we ask God for forgiveness, immediately, as we repent and God knowing that we are sincere, He forgives us immediately. Therefore, it is not right to hold another person in contempt until we make up our mind whether we should forgive or not. Let's remember the one who did the wrong is also a child of God.

Also realizing that as individuals we also offend others, and we are not immune to causing hurt to another. Therefore, we are also expected to apologize when we offend someone. James 5:16(KJV) says, "Confess your faults one to another, and pray one for another, that ye may be healed. The effectual fervent prayer of a righteous man availeth much." In our humanity we remember all the wrongs done toward us, but when the shoe is on the other foot, and we have committed an offence against our colleague or a family member etc., we fail to feel that we should apologize. But even so we should prayerfully press to apologize and be quick to do it, because this also frees us. I remember a believer once saying, that nothing is in the Word of God that we are expected to apologize to anyone. Most of us raised our children, teaching them to apologize to their siblings or friends and vice versa. It did not damage them, but it made them better adults. This does not mean that we should lose sleep if someone does not apologize to us. God will always prompt that one who should be doing the apologizing, if they refuse, it is still in God's hand, just pray for them. We cannot hate a person if we are sincerely praying for God's blessing on them. Press beyond becoming offended!

We give the whole act of injustice done to us, to God when we forgive those who did us wrong. He will deal with the situation in ways we cannot comprehend. Remember the person who hurt us, is also a child of God, so we should be praying for their deliverance and that God gives us the fortitude and understanding to press through the experience in love. "Put on therefore, as the elect of God, holy and beloved, bowels of mercies, kindness, humbleness of mind, meekness, longsuffering: Forbearing one another, and forgiving one another, if any man have a quarrel against any: even as Christ forgave you, so also do ye. And above all these things put on charity, which is the bond of perfectness." (Colossians 3:12-14(KJV) When God forgives us, as He always does, He wipes the slate clean and does not remember the wrong we did anymore.

As Believers we sometimes wonder why we go through so many trials, when all we've been doing is seeking to walk in a correct manner before God. Even as it may be true, to be in the army of the Lord, one must be trained at each level. God trains and makes His Soldiers ready. Being a Believer does not prevent one from facing trials or making mistakes. "If ye then be risen with Christ, seek those things which are above, where Christ sits on the right hand of God. Set your affection on things above, not on things on the earth. For ye are dead, and your life is hidden with Christ in God." (Colossians 3:1-3(KJV) Forgiveness is an act of the heart, not personal feelings, but through faith believing. Forgive and be free!

Fear - Now the enemy will seek to make you fearful and because you're so tired of getting hurt that you begin to protect yourself from the onslaught of mistreatment coming from the enemy through those who allow themselves to be used by him. Being vulnerable to others is out of the question, the encouragement to you is to believe what God has said, as the Word tells us that, "There is no fear in love; but perfect love casts out fear: because fear has torment. He that fears, is not made perfect in love." (1 John 4:18(KJV) People can experience fear that bring suspense, as well as fear that is helpful, which is good fear. The fear that brings anxiousness causes damage to your spirit. If one allows the actions of others to make them fearful, then they lose courage to take a stand for themselves and those they love. This causes one to behave in a cowardly manner and not stand against wrongs done to themselves or others. Whether it's a loved one, a co-worker or anyone else in trouble we should press through fear and help them. "For we wrestle not against flesh and blood, but against principalities, against powers, against the rulers of the darkness of this world, against spiritual wickedness in high places." (Ephesians 6:12(KJV) Being afraid to stand up for what is right can allow a crime to be committed against another in our presence and because we fear for our life, we fail to report what we've witnessed to the Authorities, even as we know God has promised to be with us. We have been called to be lights in the earth and to be quiet displays selfishness causing evil and unfairness to fester. When we stand up, with trust in the Lord, He will take care of us and shield us from danger. "Behold, I give you power to tread on serpents and scorpions, and over all the power of the enemy: and nothing shall by any means hurt you." (Luke 10:19KJV)

Then there is a good kind of fear, which is to, ".... fear God and keep His Commandments. (Ecclesiastes 12:9(KJV)" We will live with Him someday and escape damnation through our obedience to His Word.

When we help someone in the face of fear even as we're also afraid, know that He will keep us when we trust Him by faith. Indeed, the Lord gives wisdom to allow us to get through what is happening around us. "The fear of the Lord is the beginning of wisdom." (Proverbs 9:10(KJV) We are expected to be like Jesus, who stood for what was right, even though He knew He would be crucified. Jesus called people including the scribes and pharisees, hypocrites as they were saying one thing and living another and He did not try to smooth over their wrong-doing because He was afraid to hurt their feelings. "Stand therefore, having your loins girt about with truth, and having on the breastplate of righteousness." (Ephesians 6:14(KJV) Our example, be courageous.

Panic, Anxiety, Depression, – These three symptoms even though different, occur when one goes through difficult and unfortunate times. Although different these are also Mental Health issues which stem from high stress. **Panic** is seen as, fear when we let it get out of control. It usually lasts for a few minutes and cannot be explained, except that the person is suddenly overwhelmed by fright. But the Lord's Word says, "Fear thou not for I am with thee: be not dismayed: for I am thy God: I will strengthen thee; yea, I will help thee; yea I will uphold you with the right hand of my righteousness" (Isaiah 41:10(KJV). **Anxiety** can be the result of worry or fear which many times may or may not be mixed with sin, e.g. Jacob returning home after many years away, and is anxious because he stole the birthright from his brother Esau. Now he sees Esau's Caravan approaching and anxiety sets in. (Genesis 32:6,7(KJV). Hannah was anxious, not because she sinned, but she wanted to conceive a child which did not quickly happen. Hanna knew, because of the laws of the time in which she lived, it was important to have a man child. (1 Samuel Chapter1). God's Will is, that we trust Him, as The Holy Spirit stays with us to see us through. **Depression** can attack anyone regardless to their station in life, rich or the poor, and occurs when one is broken hearted or seriously crushed in spirit, either from the death of a loved one or loss of business, a job or worse. "The Lord is nigh unto them that are of a broken heart; and saves such as be of a contrite spirit" (Psalm 34:18(KJV). He will never leave or forsake you, continue to trust Him.

Bitterness, Anger, Resentment – When you allow what has happened or transpired in your life, which comes from hurt, or when someone has said nasty things to cause you to be so angry that you begin to allow your inner self to feed on the anger, thereby not forgiving, this turns into resentment. Then you tell your story over and over to anyone who would dare listen. Thus, your feelings move on to bitterness, especially when you know that whatever they did or said about you was untrue, intentional and mean-spirited. I speak from my personal experience, which I had to catch hold of early, thanks be to Father God. I was able to press into the joy of the Lord, which came through much study of the Word of God, high praise and continual forgiveness. That's not to say you have not been hurt and you do talk about it because you are pained. If what you have experienced is not positively dealt with quickly, these feelings move on to bitterness. A person who is either, angry, resentful or bitter, constantly snaps at others for the least little thing, hurling insults at persons close to them for no apparent reason. Bitterness can also cause illnesses to begin in your body when one allows any of these feelings to fester within the spirit. It can be detrimental or cause one to do what was never intended. The enemy can take you out on a limb, as his intention is to leave you if you should fall into that which is regrettable, or a point where he thinks there is no return for you. His intention is to destroy you in the first place. "Follow peace with all men, and holiness without which no man shall see the Lord: looking diligently lest any man fail of the grace of God; lest any root of bitterness springing up trouble you, and thereby many be defiled." (Hebrews 12:14,15(KJV).

Be careful not to allow offences to seep deeply into your spirit and begin to replay them over and over in the mind and as I stated earlier, we want to tell our hurt story over and over which usually ramps up the anger, resentment and bitterness. The enemy knows once he gets an inroad into our spirit, he seeks to ensure that we never let it go. But the only way we can experience healing is to forgive. God requires that we forgive, as Jesus already bore our pain when He was crucified on the cross. God cares for us, as well as those who hurt us, therefore let's give it to Him, because we only hurt ourselves when we hold on to anger, resentment and bitterness. God sees the whole picture and will bring the healing that is necessary. "And be kind one to another, tenderhearted, forgiving one another, even as God for Christ's sake hath forgiven you." (Ephesians 4:32(KJV) Forgiving others is healthy!

Living in Love – The Bible at 1 Corinthians 13:5(KJV) explains that, God is love and He is not out to punish you or bring you down to shame and disgrace. Love is honest, not rude or arrogant and never makes sure to get its own way. Neither does love record all the wrongs they feel was done against them, or compare themselves to others, but lives by example. Love depends on the Word of God to judge and follow actions that are true and correct. This means that love does not walk in pride. "For whom the Lord loveth He chasteneth and scourges every son whom He receives." (Hebrews 12:6(KJV) Our God wants the very best for us, and there are rewards that come from the pursuits of loving those around us. It comes through our seeking Him, listening for His Voice and pressing into faith.

This gives us the understanding that The Holy Spirit stands alongside us to keep us from evil. "But without faith, it is impossible to please Him: for he that cometh to God must believe that He is, and that He is a rewarder of them that diligently seek Him." (Hebrews 11:6(KJV) The word 'love' is used so loosely these days, but if we truly love it should be easy to share God's love with others, so they too can have a right to Salvation when they discover that He loves them too. Our love for God should shine out so that others see His love in our lives, e.g. when you can unselfishly step in to help someone who may have caused trouble for you, with no strings attached, this is God's love shining in you. His love is shown in the earth when we can love another. To be an influence on someone else's life, you must show them love and it should always extend beyond just words. People know when they feel genuine love or merely pretense. Even when we do missions for the needy, e.g. a home for disadvantaged children. They know if they are only being tolerated until after your visit with them is over, because it is spirit, and they can easily feel either your love, or fear and or resentment of them.

Both love and hate release a different presence into the atmosphere, which builds upon the thoughts and conversations affecting those involved. You may walk into a room and feel the spirit of love or hate coming from the occupants. You have heard it said, you could've cut the atmosphere in that room with a knife. "Fear thou not; for I am with thee: be not dismayed; for I am thy God: I will strengthen thee; yea, I will help thee; yea, I will uphold thee; yea, I will help thee with the right hand." (Isaiah 41:10(KJV) Show kindness and warmth to all, even to those who are not kind and warm to you. Loving others despite what we feel personally, pleases God and it's how our great reward comes in. Love and humility truly give us power to walk in the Divine Destiny that God has purposed for us. "For God hath not given us the spirit of fear; but of power, and of love, and of a sound mind." (2 Timothy 1:7(KJV)

Walking through life, Resisting Temptation - you are sure to encounter obstacles in life and some may seem insurmountable, but when you know that God is with you every step of the way, the journey becomes much lighter. It has been said, the quickest path from one point to another, is a straight line. When the path is crooked, there are many dangerous twists and turns that can easily lead you off the right path, and if you're not careful one can easily make a wrong turn. The Holy Spirit's desire is that we stay on the right course, thus making a difference.

Our blessing through it all is that The Holy Spirit, walking alongside us keeps us from going astray. The best decision is to stay on the straight and narrow. Once we trust Him, we will remain on the right course. The enemy continuously lurks around to lead you away from the right path. Proverbs 3:5-6(KJV) says, "Trust in the Lord with all thine heart; and lean not unto thine own understanding. In all thy ways acknowledge Him, and He will direct thy paths." Trusting in The Lord with all your heart, helps you give the worries and frustrations in our heart (mind), to Him. The Word tells us to cast all our cares on the Lord, for He cares for us. Trusting in The Lord rather than any other religion or sect is a tried and proven principle. From the Old Testament beginning from the Creation throughout the New Testament to Revelation, the entire Word of God outlines endless testimonies of Miracles and Promises for the people of God. Yes, The Bible is filled with miracles, so all Glory belongs to The Lord for orchestrating it all to happen. Clear miracles that God performed include, the birth of Jesus Christ into the world; Saving the three Hebrew boys, Shadrach, Meshach, and Abednego in the fiery furnace; David killed Goliath with a little pebble and a slingshot, to name a few.

There are thousands of people with testimonies of healings, and all kinds of other miracles from deliverance, spiritual guidance, to financial increase, they know only The Lord could have done for them. There are many miracles that He's done in my own life. One example is protection over my family, when we knew we were in danger. It was a time when in our city the electricity would be cut off by the Electricity Company for short periods with no warning. One night it was off a little longer than usual and one of my young children asked for a snack, so we went to the kitchen, my son who was older, held the lighted lantern. It is good we did go to this part of the house, because we heard someone tampering with the front door lock. At first, I froze, but then I remembered I could not show my fear, as that would frighten the children even more, as my daughter began holding tightly onto me. So, I shouted out aloud, whoever you are, try it and see what happens to you. Then I began to throw things around out of the cupboard, as if I was taking out my weapon planning my protection against whoever it was. Even though I did not know what I would do if they did get in, but I kept praying, asking

God's help. Suddenly, the noise at the door stopped and whatever they were poking around the lock with stopped and they left the porch. I peeked out and did not see anyone in the dark. The next day, I told the neighbor closest to our house what happened. We knew they had someone from another country who was visiting. After that incident, we never saw that visitor anymore. It seemed they got rid of him right away.

To be Tempted is also a part of living. We know Adam and Eve was tempted by the serpent, and they did not pass the test God had given them and ate the forbidden fruit (Genesis 3:1-24(KJV). Jesus was tempted by the devil, while He was fasting, but He rebuked him saying, 'get thee behind me', and Jesus passed this test (Luke 4:1-13(KJV). The example by Jesus, lets us know that we too can overcome. Temptation is not sin, but merely the enemy's tactics to ensnare us, as he paints a picture in our mind to appear real. Then when we follow the enemy's leading and do what he says, that becomes sin and we are left ashamed. Never allow the enemy to lead you away through the mind, causing you to believe this is the way to go.

Temptations can be, seeking to get ahead in life thereby joining in unscrupulous deals for extra money; becoming sexually promiscuous, whether married or single; living in pride, which is attached to selfishness where one only highlights his own achievements, rather than giving God thanks. Never allow the enemy to lead you from God's presence. Therefore, it is important that your priorities are in the right place. "Wherefore let him that thinketh he standeth take heed lest he fall. There hath no temptation taken you but such as is common to man: but God is faithful, who will not suffer you to be tempted above that ye are able; but will with the temptation also make a way to escape, that ye may be able to bear it (1 Corinthians 10:12-13(KJV)." Allow the Holy Spirit to guide you!

Disobedience – When we walk in a spirit of disobedience, it makes it difficult for one to hear what God is saying to us within our spirit.

If one has received the gift of the Holy Spirit, we should keep our spirits open to hear when God is speaking to us. There are indeed instructions that the Lord would give even for daily interactions with family and colleagues. Someone may be speaking to you in a way you think is rude, you may be preparing to give a strong come-back from your own lips. The Holy Spirit says to you in His Still small Voice, do not answer, but you answer and then a big word battle happens between the two of you. We know that when anger is caused, very harsh, insulting words have been spoken and the situation gets out of control. Or someone gets more upset and tells you that the whole situation was your fault, then you become guilty. You would have missed this whole situation if you had only listened to the voice of the Holy Spirit. Then you realize your mistake and you are the one needing to apologize. If the Holy Spirit told you do not answer in the first instance, He would have revealed to you how to deal with the matter. "Submit yourselves therefore to God, resist the devil, and he will flee from you. (James 4:7(KJV)

Christians can also find themselves getting caught up in activities that they never intended, or where it is not directly spelt out in the Bible, whether it is wrong. Some of these are the smoking of tobacco or other substances, drinking alcoholic beverages or ingesting illegal substances. To indulge in this type of behavior should not be followed by Christians, even as it is done socially at parties or special events. This is where one should ask the Lord, should I attend this event, or not. The Holy Spirit will tell you whether you are to go to a function or not. But many have been embarrassed when they have not listened to the Holy Spirit's leading. "Wine is mockery, strong drink is raging: and whosoever is deceived thereby is not wise." (Proverbs 20:1(KJV)

The Bible says, "...lean not unto thine own understanding." (Proverbs 3:5(KJV) Remember we talked about the Holy Spirit being our Helper and walking alongside us to impart the necessary wisdom while waiting for His Leading. Some years ago, I was one of the persons at my job selected to attend a Conference at an exclusive venue. The only problem, those who were scheduled to go were not told until the morning of the event. Our head of Department was only advised of this by her superior on the evening before which was after the office had closed for the day. So around 8:30 a.m. the next morning, I was given the news, which meant I would have had to leave immediately as The Conference was to begin at 9:30 a.m. What was significant about all of this was that early in the morning while preparing for work, I decided to dress casually as it was the end of the week and I had planned to remain at my desk all day to complete most of the work on my desk as possible. I remember the Holy Spirit whispering to my spirit, "Take a jacket." So naturally, I paid no attention to His still small voice and went ahead and wore casual clothes. That is where my act of disobedience occurred, because I do remember answering believing I was talking to myself saying, I don't need a jacket, I am not going to be in any meetings today." I would have been content dressed casually if I had just taken a jacket. I felt uncomfortable, as everyone was dressed professionally. Now no one at the conference looked at me strange, but I knew that had I worn a jacket I would have been more comfortable.

When the Holy Spirit is speaking to you, drawing something to your attention, regardless to how frivolous it may seem, always pay attention and be obedient, never ignoring what He is saying to your spirit. This shows that God is concerned about our every little matter. Just as we as parents are concerned about our baby's every little whimper. He knew I would not have wanted to show up to a conference dressed like this. Because I disregarded His Still Small Voice and was disobedient, I had to ask God for forgiveness. He wants to be a part of our whole life whatever we are doing. I had learnt a hard lesson.

"If ye abide in me and my words abide in you, ye shall ask what ye will and it shall be done unto you." (John 15:7(KJV) In a home when parents are raising young children, many times they reward their children with good gifts, sometimes it may be an extra privilege when the child is obedient, and rewards for disobedience in the form of a learning experience which often means a privilege is taken away for a while for disobedience, or for not doing well at school etc. To abide in the Lord, is to be obedient by Faith to what The Word of God says. This means that we believe Him by faith. "And this is the confidence that we have in Him, that, if we ask any thing according to His Will, He hears us. And if we know that He hear us, whatsoever we ask, we know that we have the petitions that we desired of Him. (1 John 5:14-15(KJV) Therefore, when we ask God to do something for us, by faith we receive. **Our obedience releases His Promises to us.**

God requires only that we **believe Him** and expects that we trust Him completely. We do not fully understand everything, but when we do not act on what we believe, most likely what we have asked for does not come to pass. Apply the Word of God to our life, "Now Faith is the substance of things hoped for, the evidence of things not seen." (Hebrews 11:1) When we believe the word, and what God has said in His promises, this is our faith being built up, and strengthening our confidence in God. "Verily, Verily, I say unto you, He that heareth my word, and believeth on Him that sent me, hath everlasting life, and shall not come into condemnation; but is passed from death into life." (John 5:24(KJV) My experience has been that when I read the Word of God aloud, my faith is strengthened, because then I remember more of what I have read. We can stand in faith believing, knowing He will be with us in whatever we face. "Who is he that overcometh the world, but he that believeth that Jesus is the Son of God?" (1 John 5:5(KJV)

Guarding the Tongue - As Christians, one of our main responsibilities is to guard our tongue. "Even so the tongue is a little member, and boasteth great things. Behold, how great a matter a little fire kindleth! (James 3:5(KJV)" Dr. Charles Stanley describes the tongue as a weapon that can cause mass destruction near and far, causing wars between countries; death in families, marriages, relationships, close churches and businesses, none is exempt when the tongue is not guarded. The tongue can also destroy governments, hope for people, someone's reputation, a career, just to name a few. One way to describe having an unguarded tongue is gossiping. The Bible says, "The words of a talebearer are as wounds, and they go down into the innermost parts of the belly. (Proverbs 26:22(KJV)" Many persons believe that only women gossip, but in my experience, I have also seen men who gossip. Gossipers seem to have a way of seeking out information of a private nature about others and disclosing it in circles that would hurt or bring shame by highlighting their short-comings and what they perceive as faults about that one, hence causing embarrassment and pain. The aim is to appear more superior than the one they have targeted, thus, changing information on a situation to seem more negative to suit their own purposes. "Being filled with all unrighteousness, fornication, wickedness, covetousness, maliciousness; full of envy, murder, debate, deceit, malignity; whisperers," (Romans 1: 29(KJV) Gossiping and lying can go together as these types of people usually craft their accounts of situations by stretching a narrative. This is a terrible evil, which causes serious trouble even for the one doing it, as they often lack proper judgment, which leaves others emotionally wounded. Gossip can be the reason for separation of family, friends and colleagues. "A talebearer reveals secrets: but he that is of a faithful spirit conceals the matter." (Proverbs 11:13(KJV)

Always bear in mind and keep close to your heart, that what you say, forms your life. Psalm 19:14(KJV) tells us to, "Let the words of my mouth and the meditation of my heart, be acceptable in thy sight, O Lord, my strength and my redeemer." The proper use of the tongue has caused people to live in peace within the law of the land as well as before God. "Death and life are in the power of the tongue: and they that love it shall eat the fruit thereof. (Proverbs 18:21(KJV) Our words should be in accord with what God has said regarding us as He wants good things for us. Even if God's Words seem too good to be true e.g. "And the Lord shall make thee the head, and not the tail; and thou shall be above only, and thou shall not be beneath; if thou harken unto the commandments of the Lord thy God, which I command thee this day, to observe and to do them:" (Deuteronomy 28:13(KJV) This tells us that when we follow God's Commandments, He will exalt us. When you speak positively about yourself and others, it remains planted in the heart.

Also, when you know that the word says, "But there is a spirit in man: and the inspiration of the Almighty giveth them understanding." (Job 32:8(KJV) These are words that can grow on you, and indeed give you the fortitude you need to take you through times of difficulty, even if there was a serious prognosis from the doctor; you feel there is eminent danger around you; or just surviving any situation which you may confront. Know in your heart, that your words can deliver you from danger, and whenever God says something, it is truth, and will surely come to pass as only the truth of His Word makes one free to succeed. If someone is seriously ill and feels that their health will not improve, to speak words of encouragement and strength will give hope rather than agreeing with them when they believe the worst may happen for them. Words of doubt remains in the spirit and soul. But the Word says, "It is the spirit that quickeneth: the flesh profitheth nothing: the words that I speak unto you, they are spirit, and they are life. (John 6:63 (KJV)" Allow the Words that God says to remain within you!

The Lord is aware of our every nuance and hears every word we speak. This can be frightening when we think of all the terrible words we have spoken about others, and even of ourselves be it in jest or not. The judgmental criticisms whether fair or unfair as we may believe, as well as all the hateful, angry, careless, vain, nasty words. Have you ever had cruel words spoken to you by someone you loved, or at you as soon as you got in earshot of others and they all laughed? Or have entered a room while a conversation was going on and you immediately understood you were the recipient of what their thoughts really were of you. Then when they realized you were present, they tried to change the subject, or even apologized by saying they were only joking. You may have tried to act as if you did not care, but oh the awful feeling that little ordeal caused within your spirit. Those words are still alive within your soul, as well as in the souls of the persons who said them. Because once words are spoken in the atmosphere, whether good or bad they cannot be retrieved. Even if you were the one playing devil's advocate and speaking cruel words of another. Before we even speak about making comments about any matter, we should make it a habit to think it through before we open our mouth. "If thou hast done foolishly, in lifting up thyself, or if thou hast thought evil, lay thine hand upon thy mouth." (Proverbs 30:32) Regardless of which side of the conversation you are on, whether you are the one to apologize or the one to forgive, do it right now and become the recipient of God's Divine Healing.

Words should be used to encourage and may include, God bless you, I'm praying for you, I'll help you, you're beautiful today, don't worry about it, I'm sorry, I misspoke, things will get better soon, God cares, I love you, I believe in you, You're always blessed. There are many, many positive words we can speak that blesses another, as well as ourselves. The truth is, just as nasty words remain in our spirit and soul, good words also remain with us. Good words bring joy, because these add to the way you feel and remains planted within your heart. This is the reason why persons love to be around those who speak positive words to them, and they shun persons with negative, hurtful words. I've heard some Christians say, that's just the way I am, I say things as I see it, or even go so far as to say that the Lord told them to say such degrading things about another one of His children. "… for out of the abundance of the heart the mouth speaketh." (Matthew 12:34(KJV)

If the Holy Spirit has placed within your heart, to speak a word of caution or correction to one of his children, then you should first prayerfully prepare yourself, and never make a scene about it, or draw attention to yourself or the one you're to speak to. Then you should truly allow Him (the Holy Spirit) to guide you, because this is another one of God's children and you do not want to be on the end of being accused of trying to cause trouble for that one. "But I say unto you, that every idle word that men shall speak, they shall give account therefore in the day of judgement. For by thy words thou shalt be justified, and by thy words thou shalt be condemned." (Matthew 12:36-37(KJV) We must also be aware that what we say should come from the heart. One may speak words that they very quickly regret because it has caused great stress, disagreements, friendships lost forever, pain and much suffering or the revealing of important or private information that someone does not wish to be spoken of so carelessly. Therefore, let's understand that when words that should not have ever been spoken, are uttered they can never be retrieved, and can leave great pain and unnecessary distress. "Even so the tongue is a little member, and boasts great things. Behold, how great a matter a little fire kindleth!" (James 3:5(KJV)

We have all experienced embarrassment at some point in our lives, when we have said the wrong words at the wrong time and realized the great pain we had caused. I can tell you, just saying sorry does not always cut it when we have carelessly damaged another. When we allow the Holy Spirit to clean up our hearts (Psalm 51:10(KJV) and 'renew a right spirit within', which only comes from having personal experiences through interactions such as have been spoken of above and learning from them. To speak good words to another especially when they are going through sorrow or hardship, even a small child who needs to hear they are going to be great when they grow up, brings hope to them. The Word says at Proverbs 20:27(KJV), "The spirit of man is the candle of the Lord, searching all the inward parts of the belly." To instill positive thoughts within a child at an early age, will further cause him to have positive behaviors and attitudes that will surely be seen at school. Good words keep others grounded like an anchor holding a boat in place, this brings hope. People of every age and walk press for the positive and gain success in life. "With long life will I satisfy him and shew him My salvation." (Psalm 91:16(KJV) Positive words bring blessing and good success. Pray like this:

> Dear Lord, teach me how to guard my tongue when speaking and interacting with others. If I am angry, intimidated or afraid, show me how to allow the

Holy Spirit to guide me as I follow the words of Psalms 141:3(KJV), "Set a watch O' Lord, before my mouth, keep the door of my lips." Teach me patience to deal with hard situations Lord! Amen!

Shun Slander and Accusation: These are acts that are always done maliciously against someone whom the offender (a slanderer or accuser) holds a secret jealousy or just hate. It is done in ways where the offender gets the most out of their effort to hurt the targeted person as much as possible. Slander can be disguised as gossip, but it is far worse than just gossip, which is still sin. Gossipers mainly stretch the narrative of some bad story they might have heard about someone, which is usually meant to spread quickly to bring hurt, pain and embarrassment. But the purpose of separately speaking of this topic in this segment, is so that readers may understand the difference between the two and the seriousness of slandering another. The one orchestrating the slandering doesn't need an existing story, they make up their own lies and have them told in the circles where they would do the most cutting damage, in order to cause serious harm to the targeted person usually in an effort to spoil the reputation and downfall of that one. Also, the one being targeted is most likely looked up to by others as displaying outstanding character. God does not agree with anyone lying, and therefore tells us in the Ninth Commandment, "Thou shalt not bear false witness against thy neighbor (Exodus 20:16(KJV)."

Accusation can also be used to get persons to do a thing that seems fine, like breaking the rules for what appears to be a good cause, but when the task is done, they find out later that the person vowing to cover for them was the one who orchestrated the plan, to set them up. A good example, a Supervisor is asked by a colleague to allow another person (a workman) not employed at his company to enter the premises after normal working hours to do some urgent work in one of the offices. The work may be required, but the colleague asking for the work to be done knows the standard rules and asks the Supervisor in what appears to be good faith, stating that he would stand with him (the Supervisor) in the event management had a query. But, also knowing his real plan is to be the one to inform management that an outsider was allowed on the premises after approved working hours, thus causing that Supervisor to be reprimanded, or this mistake even costing him his job. "For the mouth of the wicked and the mouth of the deceitful are opened against me: they have spoken against me with a lying tongue (Psalm 109:2(KJV)." The purpose is to cause the damaged Supervisor to be viewed as careless and not to be trusted in such an important role. Also, the employee may have been coveting the Supervisor's job the whole time.

In the New Testament, the Pharisees knew that Jesus would heal the man with the withered hand whether it was the Sabbath Day or not, they therefore plotted to watch Him do it, so they could find reason to accuse Him. "And, behold, there was a man which had his hand withered. And they asked Him, saying, is it lawful to heal on the Sabbath days? That they might accuse Him! (Matthew 12:10)." This was done so that they could form a slanderous case against Him, which would lead to His Crucifixion. This was slanderous persecution, and many Believers are persecuted this way, even today. "Blessed are they which are persecuted for righteousness sake: for theirs is the kingdom of heaven, blessed are ye, when men shall revile you, and persecute you, and shall say all manner of evil against you falsely, for my sake. Rejoice and be exceeding glad: for great is your reward in heaven: for so persecuted they the prophets which were before you." (Matthew 5:10-12(KJV)

Slander is a work which begins in the heart which is usually thought out and carefully planned. Therefore, this is an egregious sin and an act of making false statements to damage a person's reputation. People normally work all their life to make a good name for themselves and build a good character. A slanderer can speak one false accusation about another thus destroying the character of that one in minutes. "A good name is rather to be chosen than great riches, and loving favor rather than silver and gold." (Proverbs 22:1(KJV) Slanderers search for what may appear to be past wrongdoings or what seems to be dirt on the one they hate, seeking to use it against them, never caring whether the information is true or false. Slander is just what it is, slander, and often leaves serious negative effects regardless to whom the victims are. Believers should not be involved in acts of slander by encouraging or entertaining others with salacious jokes or tales about another. Neither should they be involved in upholding the destruction and the tarnishing of another's character.

God will judge you, as He cares for all His children. This is the reason He made the Holy Spirit available to each of us, to test the spirit and see if it is of God, "Beloved, believe not every spirit, but try the spirits whether they are of God: because many false prophets are gone out into the world." (1 John 4:1(KJV)

Secretly bitter people who may see nothing exciting happening in their own life but believe a higher promise is evident in the life of another person, usually another Believer and they, out of anger and jealousy would target them. It may be that, the Believer's children seem to be doing well in areas they wish their own children to excel. Or the person they hate seems to be a bit more gifted spiritually or professionally, which is a gifting from God, as He alone gives giftings. If you are slandered, your best defense is to trust in God's protective power.

Live Godly seeking never to follow the actions and whims of your hater, who seeks to assault your total moral character. "Whoso privily slandereth his neighbor: him will I cut off: him that hath an high look and a proud heart will not I suffer. Mine eyes shall be upon the faithful of the land, that they may dwell with me: he that walketh in a perfect way, he shall serve me. He that worketh deceit shall not dwell in my house: He that telleth lies shall not tarry in my sight. (Psalm 101:5,6,7(KJV)" God is watching our behavior and even if it is one whom we know have attacked us through slander, we naturally feel we do not care for their friendship, because of past bad experiences, let's be careful not to fight against them with our words. "Bless them that curse you and pray for them which despitefully use you (Luke 6:28(KJV)." Believers fight their battles through prayer and forgiveness, otherwise God will judge us.

Good character of believers is tested by how they treat those who may have hurt, even slandered them. "For we know him that hath said, vengeance belongeth unto Me, I will recompense, saith the Lord, and again, the Lord shall judge His people. (Hebrews 10:30(KJV)" We should place all wrongdoing toward us into God's Hand. A good test of our character is how we treat our enemies as God's Will is that we walk in righteousness, not seeking to slander anyone because we know He is working on our behalf. "Thou preparest a table before me in the presence of mine enemies: Thou anointest my head with oil, my cup runneth over (Psalm 23:5(KJV)."

Adversity is meant to bring much inward pain and it is bound to happen regardless to how one tries to control it. A simple statement or act can cause adversity between friends, even if you are the guilty one. Maybe you misspoke or mishandled a matter, and you have encountered adversity from those around you. Or maybe we can experience panic and fear when we are unable to get a matter concluded. God never causes us to go through adversity, but when we do, He allows these times to strengthen us, and we grow in grace and faith. We must remember He knows the plan for each life, and what the future holds. "Peace I leave with you, my peace I give unto you: not as the world giveth, give I unto you. Let not your heart be troubled, neither let it be afraid." (John 14:27(KJV), God will never ever leave us.

Shunning Strife and Contention – During our lifetime there are bound to be times when we will fall into disagreement with someone. This will be a time where we need to forgive, rather than opening the door to further negative contention or anger, and if it persists it can lead to bodily harm or worse. The enemy would seek to subtly cause strife between you and others wherever you are, be it at home, work, church or elsewhere. Sometimes Christians can easily believe that they have the right of way to God, because they have been faithful and that He would listen to them before He even hears the other person. "But the Lord is faithful, who shall stablish you, and keep you from evil." (2 Thessalonians 3:3(KJV) God does not deal in intimidation, as to intimidate another person is sin and He does not speak when strife is being stirred up. Therefore, one should never pray in strife, as God will not punish another one of His children because you asked Him to. This is walking in pride and may cause the one who also feels abused to become angry. The Lord hears each of his children who come before Him in prayer and He does not look at what is their station in life before He answers. "For the eyes of the Lord are over the righteous, and His ears are open unto their prayers: but the face of the Lord is against them that do evil." (1 Peter 3:12(KJV) As Christians we are to reject evil, press to do that which is right and to continuously seek peace. "Let all bitterness, and wrath, and anger, and clamor, and evil speaking, be put away from you, with all malice: And be ye kind one to another, tenderhearted, forgiving one another, even as God for Christ's sake hath forgiven you. (Ephesians 4:31-32(KJV) Refrain from speaking negatively about the other party. If you have been wronged in any way, this would be a good time to forgive. "He that loveth not, knoweth not God, for God is Love." (1 John 4:8(KJV)

Now you may have prayed, seeking the Lord about how to deal with your situation and because you feel that He has not answered you have become downcast. Stay on course and do not stray away from the truth of what the Word says. God sees when evil is done to us and He will surely bring justice. "Dearly beloved, avenge not yourselves, but rather give place unto wrath: for it is written, vengeance is mine; I will repay, saith the Lord. Therefore, if thine enemy hunger, feed him; if he thirst give him drink: for in so doing thou shalt heap coals of fire on his head. Be not overcome of evil but overcome evil with good. (Romans 12:19-21(KJV)" You may also believe that you are not the one at fault. God has not left you and He loves all His children.

He is working in spirit with those to whom you have had the conflict. At the same time He is working within your spirit to show you how to interact with that one, or He would even show you what your mistakes were. "It is an honor for a man to cease from strife: but every fool will be meddling." (Proverbs 20:3(KJV) Those who love strife can also seek to get others to agree with them to prolong a fight. When you are open to listening to His instructions, He would make it plain to you. God knows exactly how each situation will end. We may feel that we're the wronged party, but when the Holy Spirit lives within and we allow Him first place, we can find out otherwise. If this should happen, then the right thing to do is to repent before The Lord as He is quick to forgive. **"Follow Peace with all men, and holiness without which no man shall see the Lord."** (Hebrews 12:14(KJV) This means that we are to live peaceably with everyone, and stand for holiness, seeking to look out for those less fortunate than us. Remain on the right side of the Lord and stay away from strife. "The beginning of strife is as when one lets out water: therefore, leave off contention, before it is meddled with. (Proverbs 17:14(KJV) How many times we've seen persons removed from certain positions, whether it was at work, church or otherwise, and within your spirit, you knew God had everything to do with it.

Reject Jealousy - In truth, jealousy is really hatred, which is sin. Jealousy is best described as being covetous. The 10th Commandment at Exodus 20(KJV) says, "Thou shalt not covet...." Covetousness is desiring to have that which does not belong to you. "Let your conversation be without covetousness and be content with such things as ye have: for he hath said, I will never leave thee, nor forsake thee." (Hebrews 13:5(KJV) Some ways one can display jealousy, are envy, anger, conceit, insecurity and fear. This negativity can develop into hate, where they literally provoke the one whom they are jealous of. Behavior of this nature could come from someone close to you, where the jealous one plots against you without your knowing. They feel you possess something which should belong to them and It can even be of a Spiritual nature.

Provocation leads to strife, where the jealous one plots through gossip or more harsher means to hurt that person so that they become a target for evil meddling. Jealousy becomes evident when someone is seen to be just as, gifted, wealthy, educated, or prominent, as the jealous person. This brings on a passionate intolerance of that one and they then begin their mission to take that one down, by deeds of belittlement or other outrageous acts usually through gossip to making them appear to be of a bad character to bring them down in the presence of others so they won't succeed in their endeavors. "Again, I considered all travail, and every right work, that for this a man is envied of his neighbor. This is also vanity and vexation of spirit. (Ecclesiastes 4:4(KJV)" The Lord is grieved when Believers allow themselves to be led by the enemy's tactics. Out of jealousy, Cain slayed Abel because God accepted Abel's offering and rejected Cain's. (Genesis Chapter 4); Joseph's half-brothers were ready to murder him, because their father loved Joseph more. (Genesis Ch. 37) Usually, the person who is targeted, wonders why so many evil things are happening to them, as the jealous one never reveals him/herself.

When you use up your time focusing on others and how well they're doing, hoping it was you doing so well. It shows you don't have time to focus on how good the Lord is to you. Jealousy reveals what is in the heart, you're either not aware or not satisfied with what you believe is the gifting God has given to you. Many persons have never asked God what their giftings are. Each one of us came to earth with Divine gifts and talent's which the Lord expects that we fulfill. He waits to direct in the right way, as we allow the Holy Spirit to change us. "A man's gift maketh room for him and bringeth him before great men." (Proverbs 18:16(KJV) One does not need to be jealous of another's gift, as God has uniquely gifted you. Allow Him to reveal it to you and embrace it.

The process of renewing the mind takes us into loving others and being kind to everyone. "Charity suffereth long and is kind; charity envieth not; charity vaunteth not itself, is not puffed up," (1 Corinthians 13:4(KJV) God loves all His children, and it is His desire that we love each other. As Christians let's seek good for each other, even if we don't know that one personally. "Thou shalt not go up and down as a talebearer among the people: neither shalt thou stand against the blood of thy neighbor; I am the Lord. Thou shalt not hate thy brother in thine heart: thou shalt in any wise rebuke thy neighbor, and not suffer sin upon him. Thou shalt not avenge, nor bear any grudge against the children of thy people, but thou shalt love thy neighbor as thyself: I am the Lord." (Leviticus 19:16-18(KJV) Let's allow the Holy Spirit to change us. He will indeed reveal our faults and in repentance we can become more like Jesus and we will find that our mind changes for the better.

KEYS TO LETTING
YOUR LIGHT SHINE

———◆◆◆———

L iving in Joy – When your heart is joyful, your countenance completely reveals it. A joyful demeanor helps the spirit, soul and body move toward healthy progress. Proverbs 17:22(KJV) tells us, "A merry heart doeth good like a medicine: but a broken spirit dries up the bones." I would like to say a merry heart, is usually the medicine that heals the heart and attitude. When the heart is satisfied, merry and at peace, it brings restoration and healing strength to us as well as to others around us, because if one is ill, and the atmosphere is permeated with sadness, then the sick one may have difficulty feeling the healing balm. That is why, when a person is very ill, the Doctor sometimes recommends that their family make sure they watch programs on television that are calming. This can even be Comedy Re-runs or even listening to upbeat music, will bring bring about a joyful spirit within them. When your spirit is broken, you can very easily lapse into depression. Depression draws on your strength, it keeps you from seeing the favorable side of where God wants to take you, and usually brings on unwanted illnesses. Be encouraged to press past depression, which takes you into a wilderness within your spirit and can lead to loneliness, fear, doubt and uncertainty. Whatever you go through in life, remember God sees you, so trust Him to lead you out.

Paul and Silas would have been headed for the last days of their lives and should have been in great depression, on being thrown in Prison and the Roman Magistrates ordering that they were to be put to death. Although they were certainly facing sure death, they refused to let fear and doubt set in. Instead, they prayed and sang to God, and the prison shook with an earthquake and everyone's chains were loosed because they trusted in God. Trusting in Him would mean that you depend on the Holy Spirit's guidance rather than making rash decisions which you can only regret later. An example of a rash decision could be that you may be experiencing unrest at work. Before you make the decision to resign from the job, talk to God and see if it is His will, because it is He, who you need to depend on to cause you to find another job. Otherwise you may be in a wilderness state longer than you wish to be. The enemy wants you to remain weak in a low state, "…be strong in the Lord and the power of His might." (Ephesians 6:10(KJV) "Then he said unto them, go your way, eat the fat, and drink the sweet, and send portions unto them for whom nothing is prepared: for this day is holy unto our Lord: neither be ye sorry; for the joy of the Lord is your strength." (Nehemiah 8:10(KJV)

Honesty In trusting God, we should be honest in our dealings, because an honest heart means you are in obedience to God. You may go into a store to purchase something and when the Cashier gives the receipt and change, you find she has given more change than she should have. Immediately the Holy Spirit prompts us to return the funds. This does not mean that God has blessed you, it is dishonesty, and it would also mean that her cash draw would be short, and she could lose her job. "Providing for honest things, not only in the sight of God, but in the sight of man. (2 Corinthians 8:21)"

Pressing to be obedient to God, means you will face conflicts with others who do not think as you do. You've heard them, it does not take all of that to be a Christian. Yes, my friend, it does take being obedient to God in all things, there's where your blessings lie. So, if the Holy Spirit speaks to you to help someone in some small way, be obedient.

"Casting down imaginations, and every high thing that exalteth itself against the knowledge of God, and bringing into captivity every thought to the obedience of Christ:" (2 Corinthians 10:5(KJV)

Be careful to wait on God for an answer to that which you have been praying about. Waiting causes discipline, patience, and maturity wihin you, as only He knows when you are ready to receive what you're asking for, so stay in His Will. Press beyond fear and anxiety, which can easily overpower your spirit. Pray constantly in the Spirit (in your prayer language) while waiting on God, because He alone knows how we should pray, and would pray through us what we should be saying to God. "But they that wait upon the Lord shall renew their strength; they shall mount up with wings as eagles; they shall run, and not be weary; and they shall walk, and not faint. (Isaiah 40:31(KJV); "And be not conformed to this world: but be ye transformed by the renewing of your mind, that ye may prove what is that good, and acceptable, and perfect, will of God." (Romans 12:2(KJV)

Let your life be a light to shine before men and Glorify God. Letting our light shine does not mean that we should be overbearing and obnoxious around unsaved persons, wearing our salvation on our sleeves. Trust me, The Holy Spirit will help you to be a witness, allow Him to do it. Also, it's not our place to remind someone of their wrongdoing and making them feel that we are above them because we know they are not where they should be spiritually. God wishes to use us, but it's not His wish that we be judge and jury over others. He alone is judge, and He will draw them to Himself. Our job is to be faithful while trusting His direction in letting our light shine. He may wish you to speak words of encouragement to someone at the Mall, or at an Executive meeting where it seems you are the only one, who knows Jesus. Are you capable of giving a Word of Encouragement without being embarrassed? The world should know that the only way to Heaven is through acceptance of Jesus as Savior but be a witness and move under the leading of the Holy Spirit, so whatever you do or say can be a testimony to lift-up the name of Jesus. "Let your light so shine before men, that they may see your good works, and glorify your Father which is in heaven. (Matthew 5:16(KJV)

God has called us to **be lights in this world.** The light draws people, whether they are saved or unsaved. When the light is on in you, others will be sure to see it, as your attitude would be one that can only draw others through the love of God. Notice if your house door is left open for just a moment and a light is shining on a table, flying insects would fly in from outside and encircle the light, flying around it. The light draws, therefore the light of His Presence within you is meant to draw others toward you. An excellent way to let our light shine for others to be drawn to God's Love, is to **keep our word.** If you promise someone to do something for them, and when the time arrives and you do not show up, then this is not a godly example. God keeps appointments, remember Daniel in the lion's den. When Daniel was thrown in the den of lions, God immediately showed up and shut the mouths of the lions (Daniel 6:22(KJV). Daniel is only one of many instances where God has shown up on time.

I remember many years ago at a time when my children were still very young, I wanted to go to a Watch Night Church Service. This is a Church Service to celebrate the bringing in of the New Year. I knew my vehicle was not working very well and had been cutting off and losing power at any time, but I prayed that God would take us safely and bring us home safely. At church a young woman, to whom I sometimes gave a ride, came over and said she needed a ride home. I did not want to say no, so I told her Okay, but I began to pray because I knew to take her home would take me a little out of the way from just driving straight home. Church was over, about 12:30a.m., and I began my long drive home but taking the young lady first, still prayerful and I must say, very fearful. Also, my children had fallen asleep and what would I do if my vehicle stopped at that hour on the road. The vehicle did all the driving and around 1:00a.m. or a little bit thereafter, I drove into my driveway. As soon as I pulled in, my car stopped immediately without my turning the key off. I knew that God Himself had safely taken us home in that vehicle and it never once lost power on the road during the drive, even when I stopped to allow the young lady to get out and wait for her to open the door to her house. "Trust in the Lord with all thine heart: and lean not unto your own understanding. In all your ways acknowledge Him, and He shall direct thy paths." (Proverbs 3:5,6(KJV)

Tithing and Giving - God requires that his people **give a tithe**, which is one tenth of what they would have received from their income. This is an acknowledgement of a debt to God. He does not force us to give the tithe, and He will not deny our going to Heaven if we refuse. But He honors our obedience, even though He does not need our money for himself. It is important that we give to the church and can share in the assistance of those in need and the upkeep of the House of God where worship services are held. When we do give the tithe, we are blessed and when we do not, Malachi 3:9 states that we live under a curse because we would have robbed God, which overshadows our lives. Our blessings from God impresses upon us to help others, including the poor.

"Bring ye all the tithes into the storehouse that there may be meat in mine house, and prove me now herewith, saith the Lord of Hosts, if I will not open you the windows of Heaven, and pour you out a blessing, that there shall not be room enough to receive it." (Malachi 3:10(KJV) His Word remains always! If you are not a tither, do you think you could be doing better in your life? Think about it, this is the only place in the Word where God promises, He will open His Windows from Heaven and pour you out a blessing that is so big, you may not have room enough to take it all in. "God is not a man that He should lie"...(Numbers 23:19(KJV). I am a witness! Tithing breaks curses of poverty from your life. Malachi 3:8(KJV) tells us, "Will a man rob God? Yet ye have robbed me. But ye say, wherein have we robbed thee? In tithes and offerings." When we give the tithe according to the Word of God we are blessed. God has promised to stop the enemy in his tracks just for you, from destroying that which you have worked so hard for.

Since God spoke of both the tithe and offering, the offering is that amount which we give to help others, those who are less fortunate than ourselves. These offerings are called freewill, because they are given freely straight from the kindness of one's heart. These funds are used to assist the less fortunate in the church and the community with food, clothing, and any area where it is most required. Freewill offerings are also used to assist in sending Missionaries to the Mission Field. Believers can also be encouraged that whatever contribution or service they give towards the smooth operation of the Worship Centre, is seen by God to be freewill offerings. This can be the Choir Ministry, Prayer Ministry, Sunday School, Evangelism Ministry, Youth Ministry etc. are also freewill offerings.

Many believe tithing is not mandatory in this modern age, because the New Testament does not emphasize it, and God only commanded the Israelites to give the tithe. "Woe unto you, Scribes and Pharisees, hypocrites! For ye pay tithes of mint and anise and cumin, and have omitted the weightier matters of the law, judgement, mercy, and faith: these ought ye to have done, and not to leave the other undone."(Matthew 23:23(KJV). The Scribes and Pharisees seemed to stress the giving of the tithe (which at the time were expensive herbs) more than rendering of service to the oppressed. Jesus told them that the greater offerings was love and mercy, which should be extended to those in need, rather than the lesser duty which was the tithe and that should also not be left undone. Matthew 6:21(KJV) says, "For where your treasure is, there will your heart be also." Our values should be spiritual not carnal and even as we enjoy God's blessings, our trust should not be physical possessions. Our treasure in heaven is justice for the less fortunate seeing that they have an opportunity to progress and getting their needs met. He is the provider of everything that we could ever obtain or achieve. This means that we should be obedient to what He requires of us, not giving or assisting others reluctantly, because

God is able to bless us more than we could ever imagine. Therefore, it is His desire, according to His Word, that we be cheerful givers. It would be beneficial to us in a huge way. What you make happen for others, God will make happen for you.

Be Compassionate - The dictionary definition for compassion is having a feeling of pity that makes you want to help or show mercy. It is simply to be merciful to someone else. Most of the time, the person you need to help is not a family member. But yes, you do have family members who are always in need of assistance, if only to help them out until they find a job, or get on their feet, as many would say. So how does one extend mercy, pity, love, and compassion towards persons in need? **Positive examples of love**, some people have never seen love and caring towards others being enacted right before their eyes. Especially when the one giving the assistance is not asking for anything in return for what they have done for others. They unselfishly reach out with a loving attitude, making sure their situation is taken care of, without reminding them of their mistakes, never asking – how did you get in this mess? Or making the statement, this is the last time I will be helping you in this way.

If someone has been experiencing difficulties whether it is stress on the job, in a business transaction, or in the family. Listen intently, give good advice and be sure to be sympathetic to the person confiding in you. Never discuss it with others as it can very easily cause contention and further hurt and frustration. "Submitting yourselves one to another in the fear of God." (Galatians 5:21(KJV) Once someone has confided in you, make it most important to give them a friendly telephone call periodically, to pray and check on them. This is **putting yourself in the other person's shoes**, as even when we go through difficulties, it is very encouraging to know that someone cares when they can say, I'll be praying for you, don't let this worry you, or You're not alone. A little hug helps to ease anxiety when one knows it was not in a self-serving manner, but came from the heart. "Bear ye one another's burdens and so fulfill the law of Christ." (Galatians 6:2(KJV) People know when others mean them well. It also helps **not to appear busy with other activities,** i.e. texting, on the telephone, or anything that may cause you to appear busy. If someone is explaining a complaint about someone else and they believe you will help, then assist, trusting God's guidance. This is when the counsellor has to really depend on the Holy Spirit's Guidance.

Be Genuine - Do not appear bored with what is being said or done about a situation that someone is explaining to you and expecting advice. Let them know you are in their corner. **Offhanded or uncaring words** would make you seem judgmental, even if you do not believe what is being said about a situation ask the Lord for guidance. "Put on therefore, as the elect of God, holy and beloved, bowels of mercies, kindness, humbleness of mind, meekness, longsuffering." (Colossians 3:12(KJV) When people are going through, they are quick to think they are not believed. Even if someone has hurt you forgive him without talking about it to others, or in such a way to let him know that it was only through the kindness of your heart that you've forgiven, thus **making the one being forgiven feel small and inferior, or even angered**. "And be ye kind one to another, tenderhearted, forgiving one another, even as God for Christ's sake has forgiven you. (Ephesians 4:32(KJV)" Christians should seek to impart feelings of self-worth toward others.

If one has been exploited, beaten up, robbed, or having had any other negative experience, **do not prejudge** by saying, what was he/she doing out so late at night, or they caused this on themselves because of the types of friends they hang around with. "And Jesus answering said, A certain man went down from Jerusalem to Jericho, and fell among thieves, which stripped him of his raiment, and wounded him, and departed, leaving him half dead." (Luke 10:30(KJV) "But a certain Samaritan, as he journeyed, came where he was: and when he saw him, he had compassion on him. (Luke 10:33(KJV) We see here the Samaritan did not question why or how the wounded man suffered this unfortunate situation. There is no need for us to judge others when we can trust the Holy Spirit to show us how to handle a difficult situation.

When one is in contention with another, person, you can assist them by giving wise counsel and reassurance that you will be praying about their matter. You will not help by saying, this is not my business and I don't want to be involved and you will not, should you not take sides. If the person complaining to you, is the guilty party, give counsel in a wise and compassionate manner, showing them how they may be at fault if they are willing to listen. "Blessed are the peacemakers: for they shall be called the children of God." (Matthew 5:9(KJV) Remember, do not take sides. It is a fact that, Christians are good natured, but there are those who take advantage of this when they observe it, by seeking unnecessary assistance. If there is a need for tangible assistance, always do so prayerfully, asking The Holy Spirit for guidance to be compassionate while also being a good steward over what God has caused you to possess. "And let us not be weary in well-doing: for in due season we shall reap, if we faint not." (Galatians 6:9(KJV) With trust in The Holy Spirit, He will prompt you if you are being taken advantage of.

God's Word teaches us that He is very gracious and compassionate, slow to anger, abounding in love and faithfulness. His Grace is unmerited favor, which we can never earn, and it is free. God is compassionate, as His people we should also seek to be compassionate to others. "For thou, Lord, art good, and ready to forgive; and plenteous in mercy unto all them that call upon thee." (Psalms 86:5(KJV) When asked the question, which is the great commandment in the Law, Jesus said, "Thou shalt love the Lord thy God with all thy heart. and with all thy soul, and with all thy mind. This is the first and great commandment. And the second is like unto it, thou shalt love thy neighbor as thyself. On these two commandments hang all the law and the prophets." (Matthew 22:37-40(KJV) If someone claims that they love God but hate their brother, they are a liar. "If a man says, I love God and hateth his brother, he is a liar: for he that loves not his brother whom he hath seen, how can he love God whom he hath not seen." (1 John 4:20(KJV(KJV) As Christians, we are automatically placed in the position to be of assistance in this world. Where prayer is required, it is our job because the Bible says, "and He spoke a parable unto them to this end, that men ought always to pray, and not to faint;" (Luke 18:1(KJV) Prayer may seem to be the easy way out for many Christians, because they can get into their prayer closets and pray, but one other purpose for which we are here on the earth is to be of assistance to those in need. It is not always in a monetary manner, but to give words of encouragement, and building up the spirit of another can be huge if they need a good word.

On the other hand there would be times when you do have to assist someone in a monetary way, "I have shewed you all things, how that so laboring ye ought to support the weak, and to remember the words of the Lord Jesus, how He said, it is more blessed to give than to receive." (Acts 20:35(KJV) I have heard Believers say, that is not my job, I am only responsible for those in my household. "Give and it shall be given unto you, good measure, pressed down, shaken together, and running over, shall men give into your bosom. For with the same measure that ye mete withal it shall be measured to you again." (Luke 6:38(KJV) It is God's intention that we understand that our purpose to be in the earth is for Mission first. This is Ministry for the Kingdom of God in itself. The reason you were afforded the privilege to work at that exclusive corporation; in Finance; that Fine hotel; at A Government Ministry; in Insurance; Engineering; or wherever else you are afforded the privilege to work it should be for mission first. Many Christians may say they want to go on Mission someday and yet fail to give assistance to those needy, underprivileged, poor persons and families in their immediate pathway, those who are physically around them, this is mission at home. As a Believer, it is your duty to assist as well as to be a witness for Him, trusting the Holy Spirit's Guidance, when you should do so, as with His Guidance you will not be disruptive to the workplace. You see, it is why it is most important that you allow Him to be your guide in keeping you on the right course.

Now unless you feel, I am telling you to give your hard-earned money to just anybody, this is not the case. There are those who take Christians for granted by taking advantage of them. They go around saying that the Lord has put them into full-time Ministry where they do not work on a secular job, then they try to get monies from you to help them to pay for their living necessities. Which is not always the case, as many times these persons are lazy and do not wish to work for an honest day's pay, and God has not spoken to them. "Beloved, believe not every spirit, but try the spirits whether they are of God: because many false prophets are gone out into the world (1 John 4:1(KJV)." People who use false statements like this are playing on the sympathies of others, and they are not loving God, but merely walking in pride and rebellion for their own purposes. This kind of behavior from God's people grieves Him. But if you have truly been called to full-time Ministry by the Lord, know that He will make a way for your life living, and will place others in your way who will be pleased to give you assistance.

Therefore, it is imperative to test the spirit to see if it is of God. This is where the Holy Spirit is most important to guide you into making the right decisions in these situations, as there would certainly be genuine persons whom the Lord has placed into full-time Ministry. Trust that the Holy Spirit will tell you who is truthful or not. "Even so hath the Lord ordained that they which preach the gospel should live of the gospel (1 Corinthians 9:14(KJV)." Pray in this way:

> Dear Lord, teach me how not to be indifferent toward one in Ministry who is experiencing financial difficulty. May your Holy Spirit guide me how to prayerfully assist them. AMEN!

Rescue The Perishing

Hymn by Fanny Crosby

⌇

Rescue the perishing, Care for the dying,
Snatch them in pity from sin and the grave.
Weep o'er the erring one, lift up the fallen.
Tell them of Jesus the Mighty to save.

CHORUS

Rescue the perishing, care for the dying,
Jesus is merciful, Jesus will save.

Tho' they are slighting Him, still He is waiting,
Waiting the penitent child to receive;
Plead with them earnestly, plead with them gently,
He will obey if they only believe.

Down in the human heart, crushed by the tempter,
Feelings lie buried that grace can restore;
Touched by a loving heart, wakened by kindness,
Chords that were broken will vibrate once more.

Rescue for the perishing, duty demands it,
Strength for thy labor, the Lord will provide;
Back to the narrow way, patiently win them;
Tell the poor wanderer, a Savior has died.

Fanny J. Crosby - 1869
https//www.christianmusicandhymns.com2019/09

God's Promises
To Us

T here are more than three thousand five hundred promises God has planned for our privilege in the Bible. "All scripture is given by inspiration of God, and is profitable for doctrine, for reproof, for correction, for instruction in righteousness." (1 Timothy 3:16(KJV) This means that when we know what we believe, there is no excuse to not living and walking holy before God. We are therefore entitled to God's promises.

Doctrine, The Holy Spirit keeps one on the right path to attend not just a church of choice, but one with correct doctrine to receive proper teaching of The Word. It is easier to follow when the Word is taught in absolute truth. Having this privilege shows one how to live godly on the earth. None should be able to put their personal interpretation on God's Word. That is why, new Christians are encouraged to attend a Bible teaching Church. "Sanctify them through thy truth: Thy Word is truth," (John 17:17(KJV)

Reproof - is when a Believer is directly rebuked for serious infractions in their Christian walk. It is an effort by others to discipline one not living an upright life. "He is in the way of life that keepeth instruction: but he that refuseth reproof erreth." (Proverbs 10:17(KJV) But ridicule can easily find its way into the Body of Christ, where they seek to fuss at each other. It does not say that the one scrutinized is perfect in their every deportment, but the Word of God teaches Believers to be on one accord, praying for each other in love, as Matthew 25:30(KJV) says, "...Verily I say unto you, inasmuch as ye have done it unto one of the least of these my brethren, ye have done it unto me. It cancels gossip, nit-picking, accusations and personal likes and dislikes for each other. "Now the God of patience and consolation grant you to be likeminded one toward another according to Christ Jesus:" (Romans 15:5(KJV)

Correction - Is being caring, while not allowing deliberate wrongdoing to continue. "For he that soweth to his flesh shall of the flesh reap corruption, but he that soweth to the Spirit shall of the Spirit reap life everlasting." (Galatians 6:8(KJV) If one corrects another, then there is the fear of backlash by others. Therefore, correcting others should not be based on speculation or hearsay, there must be proof that the facts are correct. Many persons have been known to disassociate themselves with church because of this kind of hurt, when they believe someone has spoken falsehoods against them. Jesus died on the Cross to save us and having accepted Him through salvation, we now live under His Grace and Mercy. Therefore, Holy Spirit seeking to correct us when we've gone the wrong way, prompting the conscience bringing understanding and letting us know that we need to repent and make it right with God. "And He said unto me, My Grace is sufficient for you: for my strength is made perfect in weakness. Most gladly therefore will I rather glory in my infirmities, that the power of Christ may rest upon me." (2 Corinthians 12:9(KJV) Instruction correctly imparted, leads one into the truth. "Obey them that have the rule over you and submit yourselves: for they watch for your souls, as they that must give account, that they may do it with joy and not with grief: for that is unprofitable for you." (Hebrews 13:17(KJV) To live morally correct is righteousness, and we receive God's justification. "For the Lord knows the way of the righteous, but the way of the ungodly shall perish." (Psalms 1:6(KJV); (Psalms 11:7(KJV)

Humans in their natural nature very easily break promises. "Let us hold fast the profession of our faith without wavering: (for He is faithful that promised;)" (Hebrews 10:23(KJV) He is purely Holy and never promises one thing today and changing His mind tomorrow. Even as one is never totally perfect, He loves us unconditionally. His Grace is enough, even in our weakness, He is always ready to forgive! "...all the promises of God are yea, and in Him Amen, unto the glory of God by us. (2 Corinthians 10:20(KJV)" When we begin to praise Him in fervency, honestly believing His Word, our faith grows strong in Him and maturity increases. Below are verses from the Word of God to help stay on the right course:

VICTORY OVER HARD SITUATIONS

For verily I say unto you, that whosoever shall say unto this mountain. Be thou removed, and be thou cast into the sea; and shall not doubt in his heart but shall believe that those things which he saith shall come to pass, he shall have whatsoever he saith. (Mark 11:23(KJV)

For the Lord your God is He that goes with you, to fight for you against your enemies, to save you. (Deuteronomy 20:4(KJV)

Wherefore take unto you the whole armor of God, that ye may be able to withstand in the evil day, and having done all, to stand. (Ephesians 6:13(KJV)

Cause me to hear thy lovingkindness in the morning; for in thee do I trust: cause me to know the way wherein I should walk; for I lift-up my soul unto thee. (Psalm 143:8(KJV)

PEACE, HOPE AND ENCOURAGEMENT

Peace I leave with you, my peace I give unto you, not as the world giveth, give I unto you: Let not your heart be troubled, neither let it be afraid. (John 14:27(KJV)

Be strong and of a good courage, fear not, nor be afraid of them: for the Lord thy God, He it is that doth go with thee; He will not fail thee, nor forsake thee. (Deuteronomy 31:6(KJV)

And the peace of God, which passeth all understanding shall keep your hearts and minds through Christ Jesus. (Philippians 4:7(KJV)

When a man's ways please the Lord, he maketh even his enemies to be at peace with him. (Proverbs 16:7(KJV)

WEALTH AND PROSPERITY

But my God shall supply all your need according to his riches in glory by Christ Jesus. (Philippians 4:19(KJV)

The blessing of the Lord, it maketh rich, and he addeth no sorrow with it. (Proverbs 10:22(KJV)

Honor the Lord with thy substance, and with the first fruits of all thine increase: So shall thy barns be filled with plenty, and thy presses shall burst out with new wine. (Proverbs 3:9-10KJV)

But thou shalt remember the Lord thy God: for it is He that giveth thee power to get wealth, that he may establish his covenant which he swore unto thy fathers, as it is this day. (Deuteronomy 8:18KJV)

HEALTH AND HEALING

Beloved, I wish above all things that thou mayest prosper and be in health, even as thy soul prospers. (3 John 1:2KJV)

But He was wounded for our transgressions, He was bruised for our iniquities: the chastisement of our peace was upon Him; and with His stripes we are healed. (Isaiah 53:5(KJV)

I shall not die, but live, and declare the works of the Lord. (Psalm 118:17(KJV)

Who forgives all thine iniquities; who heals all thy diseases; (Psalms 103:3(KJV)

JOY AND HAPPINESS

Thou wilt shew me the path of life: in thy presence is fulness of joy; at thy right hand there are pleasures for evermore. (Psalms 16:11(KJV)

He that handleth a matter wisely shall find good: and whoso trusts in the Lord, happy is he. (Proverbs 16:20(KJV)

My Brethren count it all joy when ye fall into diver's temptations; knowing this, that the trying of your faith worketh patience. But let patience have her perfect work, that ye may be perfect and entire, wanting nothing. (James 1:2-4(KJV)

For this cause we also, since the day we heard it, do not cease to pray for you, and to desire that ye might be filled with the knowledge of His will in all wisdom and spiritual understanding; that ye might walk worthy of the Lord unto all pleasing, being fruitful in every good work, and increasing in the knowledge of God; strengthened with all might, according to his glorious power, unto all patience and longsuffering with joyfulness; giving thanks unto the Father, which hath made us meet to be partakers of the inheritance of the saints in light: (Colossians 1:9-12KJV)

FAITH IN EVERY SITUATION

Therefore, I say unto you, what things so ever ye desire, when ye pray, believe that ye receive them and you shall have them. (Mark 11:24(KJV)

And this is the confidence that we have in Him, that, if we ask anything according to His will, He heareth us: And if we know that he hears us, whatsoever we ask, we know that we have the petitions that we desired of Him. (1 John 5:14-15(KJV)

Now faith is the substance of things hoped for, the evidence of things not seen. (Hebrews 11:1(KJV)

And all things, whatsoever ye shall ask in prayer, believing, ye shall receive. (Matthew 21:22(KJV)

(For we walk by faith, not by sight: (2 Corinthians 5:7(KJV)

GIVING TO HELP OTHERS

Give, and it shall be given unto you; good measure, pressed down and shaken together and running over, shall men give into your bosom. For with the same measure that ye mete withal it shall be measured to you again. (Luke 6:38(KJV)

Bear ye one another's burdens, and so fulfill the law of Christ. (Galatians 6:2(KJV)

For I was hungred, and ye gave me meat: I was thirsty, and ye gave me drink: I was a stranger, and ye took me in: (Matthew 25:35(KJV)

Thou shalt surely give him, and thine heart shall not be grieved when thou givest unto him: because that for this thing the Lord thy God shall bless thee in all thy works, and in all that thou puttest thine hand unto. (Deuteronomy 15:10-11(KJV)

MORE PROMISES TO HOLD ON TO

No weapon that is formed against thee shall prosper; and every tongue that shall, rise against thee in judgment thou shalt condemn. This is the heritage of the servants of The Lord, and their righteousness is of me, saith the Lord. (Isaiah 54:17(KJV)

I can do all things through Christ which strengtheneth me. (Philippians 4:13(KJV)

For God hath not given us a spirit of fear; but of power, and of love, and of a sound mind. (2 Timothy 1:7(KJV)

But ye are a chosen generation, a royal priesthood, an holy nation, a peculiar people; that ye should shew forth the praises of him who hath called you out of darkness into his marvelous light; (1 Peter 2:9(KJV)

For I know the thoughts that I think toward you, saith the Lord, thoughts of peace, and not of evil, to give you an expected end. (Jeremiah 29:11(KJV)

And whatsoever ye shall ask in my name, that will I do, that the Father may be glorified in the Son. (John 14:13(KJV)

Your Purpose - God has a purpose for each of us in the earth. Therefore, it is important to know Him personally, so when we accept Him as Savior and as we seek Him, our purpose would be made plain to us. Each of us came to earth with more than one purpose to fulfill. One purpose is to serve God and be a witness to others or work in Missions. The other purpose is one's life work or the profession chosen for life, either Medical, Engineering, Education, Religion, Hospitality, Law etc., or stay at home mom.

The Word of God does not indicate that one should be a Christian for a long time to be a witness for Christ. The Holy Spirit begins to live in you at the time you give your heart to God. "But ye shall receive power, after that the Holy Ghost is come upon you: and ye shall be witnesses unto me both in Jerusalem and in all Judea and in Samaria and unto the uttermost parts of the earth. (Acts 1:8(KJV)" In my own life, after becoming a Christian at the age of sixteen, I began to be a witness for God almost immediately. There were times when I would have dreams, where I knew God wanted me to either go to a certain area on Street Service, as it is known here in the Bahamas. My Pastor, at that time, both encouraged and supported the young people at his church to do missions. He knew I had heard from God as, I was only a timid teenager in the 1960's and knew very little about this, being brought up in the Anglican Church. He stepped in and taught the young people how to effectively witness. I became aware of verses such as Romans 10:9-10; John 3:16; Romans 3:23; Acts 4:12; Luke 19:10; and others. To be touched by God gives one a heart to want to tell it everywhere. Usually new converts feel the urge to tell everyone about Jesus. People responded some giving their heart to Jesus. It was the beginning of my witness for the Lord, and I have never stopped. Never be afraid to share the love of Jesus with others.

The Word of God puts us in right standing with Him, as we follow it. "The Lord, Your God will make you the head and not the tail; and thou shalt be above only, and thou shalt not be beneath: (Deuteronomy 28:13(KJV)." When God places one in a higher position (above only) means He has blessed us so that we can bless others. All that we need, both spiritually and materially, comes from Him. Deuteronomy 28: 1–14, literally outlines our inheritance in Him and in order to inherit what rightfully belongs to us, is obedience to how and what He has commanded that we do. This pleases Him! When He died on the Cross for us, Jesus became our Advocate and pleads the case on your behalf before God, reminding The Father that He gave His Life for you, hence your redemption from sin. This gives us the power to live successfully in this world. "My little children, these things write I unto you, that ye sin not, and if any man sin, we have an advocate with the Father, Jesus Christ the righteous: (1 John 2:1(KJV)" We are justified because Jesus suffered for us on the Cross. Justification is right standing with God. "...The just shall live by faith! (Romans 1:17(KJV)"

"As He (Jesus) is, so are we in this world, (1 John 4:17(KJV))." This is what happens when The Holy Spirit dwells in us. We have been given the privilege to overcome sickness, adversity and whatever we face negatively. You can live above every negative situation that would arise in your life. There is no reason to allow self-pity to grow within the spirit. When you have received healing from the stress and pain you may have been enduring, it's then when you press forward to help somebody else. This brings hope to others and they will understand that they can come through too. Therefore, your testimony should be, how the Lord brought you to where you presently are, which would encourage others. Its where we also become witnesses for him. So rather than griping about that bad experience, The Holy Spirit remains with you to give you peace that will enhance your witnessing.

In any situation, The Holy Spirit is able to cause you to escape without being harmed should a crisis arise. Do not allow the enemy to intimidate you or make you ashamed of your testimony. Allow the Lord to shape you into the character He wants, from the hurts and experiences we've endured or seeking healing from the past. If you are truly an example like Jesus, you can therefore speak to adversarial encounters coming from the enemy towards you, sickness, loss, lack, loneliness, fear etc. and command and rebuke it to leave. Jesus spoke to, the lame, the dead, the fig tree, and the storm and these all obeyed Him. Negative issues that are occurring in our lives are a result of attacks from, or through Satan our adversary.

Let's Pray: Dear Lord, I thank you for the distance you have brought me. My desire is to live for you to the end. Thank you for judging my adversary, even as I forgive. Help me to stay on the right course in my life and be a witness, as others come to know you as Savior. Amen!

Whatever God promised you in His Word, you can believe it, because it works. Continue to pray in accordance with His Word. You have not strayed from the right course, because He's said, "Therefore I say unto you, What things soever ye desire when ye pray, believe that ye receive them and ye shall have them." (Mark 11:24(KJV) "Death and life are in the power of the tongue: and they that love it shall eat the fruit thereof." (Proverbs 18:21(KJV) This means, whatever we speak from our lips, can either bring blessings or curses on ourselves. When we speak negativity on ourselves and our family, whatever we speak from our lips happens. When our physical eyes begin to see failure then we easily believe nothing is happening for us. Let's be careful of our speech and allow the Lord to guide our every word, while we thank Him for the good outcome of that which we have been believing Him for.

Determined to Stay On Course

POEM BY MYRA A. COOPER

❧

Determined Is What I Will Be,
That God's Love Is Seen in Me,
Which Means I Press to do the right,
As I Live Each Day in His Sight,
Staying on Course Continually.

I'm Determined to Live Pure as Can Be,
In My Life While I Have Breath,
And to Serve Him I am Totally Free,
As He Died on The Cruel Tree for Me,
And Stay on Course Continually.

I'm Determined to be a Bright Light,
Burning Bright Both Day and Night,
That the World May Clearly See,
What the Lord Has Done in Me,
While Staying on Course Continually.

Myra A. Cooper, 2017

Remain Resolved

I n the first pages of this book you had the privilege to meet God. I am sure you now understand what an awesome, loving Father He is. Never forget, He watches over you and you're never alone. Finally, you also know and have a clearer understanding of why you believe what you understand about serving and being a witness for The Lord, and the importance of staying on the right course for the rest of your life. Make sure your resolve is to stay totally grounded. Picture yourself as a small tree in a planter, but now needing to be planted in the ground so your roots can be fully grounded with room to spread. This is the time to allow your roots to be fully grounded in God.

> Let's Pray: Father, I thank you for bringing me to this point in my walk with you. Show me how to prayerfully stay in your Word so that I may remain grounded. I denounce the devil and all his evil, subtle works against my life. I stand on the authority of God's Word, that my life remains hidden with Christ in God, as I share His Love with others. Amen!

Pray this prayer or along these lines as often as you need to.

"Put on the whole armor of God, that ye may be able to stand against the wiles of the devil. For we wrestle not against flesh and blood, but against principalities, against powers, against the rulers of the darkness of this world, against spiritual wickedness in high places. Wherefore take unto you the whole armor of God, that ye may be able to withstand in the evil day, and having done all, to stand. (Ephesians 6:11-13(KJV)." Bear in mind that, as you press to live righteously for Him the enemy will try to stop you which can show up in the form of failure in that which you put your hands to do, character assassination, or any other derailment he can. Continue to press!

Keep your spirit clean by not compromising your beliefs or holding on to strongholds. These are life issues which we hold on to that can easily hinder one from living in the truth of what the Lord intends for us. When this happens, it allows the enemy to control the mind on negative life experiences. "For though we walk in the flesh, we do not war after the flesh. (For the weapons of our warfare are not carnal, but mighty through God, to the pulling down of strongholds:)" (2 Corinthians 10:3-4(KJV) A good example is if a Christian continues to drink alcohol even after he/she becomes saved. Alcohol causes incontinence in the mind, where one can behave in a way unbecoming a Christian. "Wine is a Mocker strong drink is Raging: and whosoever is deceived thereby is not wise." (Proverbs 20:1(KJV) This hinders the witness to promote the cause for Him.

A stronghold may also be something that has been devastating in one's life that it lingers in the spirit. Therefore, not forgiving wrongs committed against you or a loved one, can easily become a stronghold. "And when ye stand praying, forgive, if ye have aught against any: that your Father God may forgive you your trespasses (Mark 11:25(KJV)." To not forgive hinders one from serving God completely while they are holding a grudge. This reveals they are not living by the Word of God, hence finding it difficult to be at peace with others as well as themselves. This holds one back from walking in the fullness of what God has Promised. "I can do all things through Christ, which strengtheneth me." (Philippians 4:13(KJV) You get through mistakes, temptations, frustrations, and uncertainties, as many times one can easily become confused. But you find yourself getting through by continual prayer and strength which comes from the study of The Word of God. Also talking it out with a mature Christian whom you trust, who will also pray with you until you are able to stand more strongly while attending a church that teaches from The Bible. Of course, your church attendance is important, as it is a means of meeting and working with others in the gospel, who aim to stay on course like yourself.

Even as one may continue to verbally describe hard experiences which has happened to them, God has a plan where we can live beyond frustration. We fight within our minds by internalizing hard situations that has happened which may have caused depression; with the tongue by rehearsing it repeatedly causing anger and fear; then there is bitterness that grows within the spirit. Now we do not go to war like the world, where we would have to use physical armor. "Stand therefore, having your loins girt about with truth, and having on the breastplate of righteousness. And your feet shod with the preparation of the gospel of peace: Above all, taking the shield of faith wherewith ye shall be able to quench all the fiery darts of the wicked. And take the helmet of salvation, and the sword of the Spirit, which is the Word of God." (Ephesians 6:14-17(KJV) The Apostle Paul taught that putting on the Armor of God is a mindset, where we know that we are covered wherever and whenever the enemy attacks.

Before God, we are each a work in progress! Run your race with patience, and you will complete the course that is in His Divine Plan for life. Keep in mind that the race is not to the swiftest, neither to the quickest, but to those that endure to the end. Paul reminded Timothy and made him understand that even though God has appointed you, God does not always allow you to be in an area of witness that is easy. It is the enemy's intention to see that you would be persecuted, and you will be in many instances, as it is a means to cause your spiritual growth to collapse. "Thou therefore, my son, be strong in the grace that is in Christ Jesus." (2 Timothy 2: 1(KJV)

When I became a Christian many years ago, I visited some of my family member's homes in Nassau, to make sure that I had told them about Jesus. That did not go over very well, and some made me understand, that I was not to come to their home again, if I was visiting to say to them that if they did not accept Jesus as Savior, they would go to hell when they died. My family was Episcopalian, and the belief was that they were already Christians because of being a part of that church. They said I was being disrespectful, and they told my mother to make me stop. I believed I was just being a witness for Jesus, so I kept praying for them. My mom herself received the Lord many years later and is in Heaven now. Some of them later became born-again Christians. Prayer does change things!

You'll find that when you minister to others your witness should be intact once you make sure it is the right time to approach them, it's best to silently check with the Holy Spirit. Always stand on what you believe and know to be Bible based, on your own salvation, not allowing yourself to be swayed by someone else's view of what salvation should be. A clear example of this would be those who do not believe that Jesus died to become the Savior of the world. But you know that we get to heaven only through Jesus Christ. You also know there are religions that believe they get to heaven through their good works. You are bound to meet those who worship and believe differently, and do not share the same values as you do. There are many who have not come to the knowledge of Jesus' dying on the cross may find the gospel message to be offensive, depending on what they have been taught and believe. You are being prepared to be a witness wherever you go, and not just to those in the area where you live and work, so let your witness be intact and in accordance with the Word of God. At these times you will thank God for the Holy Spirit. I believe, it is truly one of the reasons why He came to earth, just to be with us. "Not by works, lest any man should boast (Ephesians 2:9(KJV)."

When you find yourself in such situations, know that The Holy Spirit is with you so remain prayerful and calm. Be reminded that you will emerge on the other end of what you are going through, and usually you'll find that He's brought you to a step higher in your walk with Him. "Know ye not that they which run in a race run all, but one receiveth the prize? So run, that ye may obtain, and every man that striveth for the mastery is temperate in all things. Now they do it to obtain a corruptible crown: but we an incorruptible." (1 Corinthians 9:24, 25(KJV) This means that we must stay in the race, because the ultimate prize is Heaven. We must run with the intention that we are the one to get the prize. We therefore cannot compare the way we run our race to how the other Believer runs, because our pattern is the Word of God, let's use it.

As we meditate on the Word and cleanse ourselves within our spirits through necessary repentance and commitment, God gives inner peace. This results in gentleness, humbleness and patience to flow from the inside out, as we learn how to monitor our thinking. As you believe that the Holy Spirit holds you and all that concerns your wellbeing, then all should be well with you. "Be careful for nothing; but in everything by prayer and supplication with thanksgiving let your requests be made known unto God (Philippians 4:6(KJV)." That is, do not be anxious but remain in patience and peace, as God has heard and will answer prayer and will indeed come through for you. The Apostle Paul did not have any finances coming in, he did not have investments, neither did he have a job, or Ministry Partners, who gave donations or sowed seeds each month to his ministry. But the Holy Spirit touched others to meet his needs. Know that God will take care of you in every situation.

We may be a witness for God, never try to be a judge of another person. God is the only Judge and if a person confesses to have received Jesus Christ as Savior, God alone knows the hearts. "If we confess our sins, He is faithful and just to forgive us our sins, and to cleanse us from all unrighteousness." (1 John 1:9(KJV) If someone has genuinely been converted, they will want to learn and understand more about Jesus. Therefore, we should invite them to church, so they can meet other

Christians, but we should not seek to turn people away from their religious beliefs. The Holy Spirit will change the heart and mind to get them to agree to eventually going to a Bible Teaching church. Our duty is to be a witness for God, we cannot save anyone. The Holy Spirit will cause them to understand that what you are saying is truth, and God Himself would do the drawing.

When we witness to others, and they are seemingly not interested, know that The Holy Spirit is working within their spirit to draw them to salvation because you planted the seed, therefore we don't have to force anyone. His job is done in love and gentleness, and at the right time He will draw them even if it is through another Believer. "I have planted, Apollos watered; but God gave the increase." (1 Corinthians 3:6(KJV) This means if one is not yet interested in giving their heart to the Lord, The Holy Spirit will have someone else bring that one in. Our job is to let others know that Jesus loves them. If we press them negatively i.e. pointing out their wrongdoing, they get angry and dig their heels in more and see Christians as self-righteous, judgmental people trying to tell them what to do with their lives. Our witness should be that, entrance into Heaven is only through Jesus Christ. We should therefore live exemplary lives before others. "Let your light so shine before men, that they may see your good works, and glorify your Father which is in Heaven (Matthew 5:16(KJV)."

We must display boldness and even as we said earlier not to force anyone, there may be times when we would have to get a bit confrontational, it must be done in love with as much gentleness as possible. The Holy Spirit will help us so that we are not fearful. Also, as pointed out earlier, we are not to force anyone, but there may be a time when the Holy Spirit urges you to speak to a person, who may be naturally an argumentative one. But if you are led by the Holy Spirit, He will guide you through any ordeal. It may be that someone is intoxicated and not behaving normally. The Holy Spirit knows where that one's life is headed, and He will urge you to speak to that one about getting their soul right with the Lord. "Have not I commanded thee? Be strong and of a good courage; be not afraid, neither be thou dismayed: for the Lord thy God is with thee whithersoever thou goest (Joshua 1:9)." Our real battle is to defeat the evil one, who fights for people's hearts and minds. The enemy does not give up what he deems his territory without a fight. The Holy Spirit will give you the wisdom in how to be a witness for Jesus. Remember He never speaks of Himself, but always points to what should be done to make Jesus known. He will direct what to say when interacting with others regarding salvation.

When you love people, just like Jesus did you will be concerned that their destination is to spend eternity in heaven. You therefore realize the need for His guidance in being a witness for Him. Our job is to plant the seed, and God would cause the increase. "So then neither is he that planteth anything, neither he that watereth; but God that giveth the increase (1 Corinthians 3:7(KJV)."

Love the Lord with all your heart and seek to be true, obeying His Word and putting Him first in everything you do. "But seek ye first the kingdom of God and His Righteousness, and all these things shall be added unto you." (Matthew 6:33(KJV)

Live with a grateful spirit every day, thanking God for all the good He continually does for you. "Enter into His Gates with thanksgiving and into His Courts with Praise: be thankful unto Him and Bless His Name (Psalm 100:4(KJV)."

Treat all Believers (as brothers and sisters) with love, patience and respect even though it may appear, they would have fallen from living an upright life and their testimony would have suffered (many would say, they have fallen from grace). When we prayerfully encourage them, God through the Holy Spirit will turn them around. "We then, as workers together with him, beseech you also that ye receive not the grace of God in vain." (2 Corinthians 6:1(KJV)

Honor and respect those having authority over you, i.e. in this case, your Pastor. He or She would be teaching, encouraging and praying that you succeed in your life and witness for Christ. When God knows you honor your spiritual leaders, He blesses your life. "Obey them that have the rule over you and submit yourselves: for they watch for your souls, as they that must give account, that they may do it with joy, and not with grief: for that is unprofitable for you." (Hebrews 13:17(KJV)

Prayer, study, meditation, obeying the Word and seeking God in everything you do. "But ye, beloved, building up yourselves on your most holy faith, praying in the Holy Ghost. Keep yourselves in the love of God, looking for the mercy of our Lord Jesus Christ unto eternal life." (Jude 20, 21(KJV)

Seek to prayerfully encourage others to live peaceably, speaking positive, encouraging things rather than criticism and anger. "These things I have spoken unto you, that in me ye might have peace. In the world ye shall have tribulation: but be of good cheer; I have overcome the world." (John 16:33(KJV)

Always seek to be honest in that which you do and say. But even as honesty is not easy, John 14:6(KJV) Jesus says, "I am the Way, the Truth, and the Life: no man cometh unto the Father, but by me." So because Jesus is honest, and we are to be like Him, then we are obligated to be honest also. Honesty should be our focus, as it is important for God does not tell lies. "My little children, let us not love in word, neither in tongue; but in deeds and in truth." (1 John 3:18(KJV)

Even as we follow God our Father and love Jesus our Elder Brother, when we believe in the truth of the Word of God there will be unity among Believers. "That they all may be one; as thou, Father art one in me and I in thee, that they also may be one in us: that the world may believe that thou hast sent me." (John 17:21(KJV)

Our attitude towards the Gospel, i.e. our assistance to others in need and the cost of the furtherance of the Gospel, God blesses us for this.

"Beloved, I wish above all things that thou mayest prosper and be in health, even as thy soul prospereth." (3 John 1:2(KJV))

When one knows better things should be happening for themselves and their family members, God has made available to you the authority to believe by faith, calling into existence that which is needed. "(As it is written, I have made thee a father of many nations,) before him whom he believed, even God, who quickens the dead, and calls those things which be not as though they were (Romans 4:17(KJV)."

Care for the young, parents, the elderly, family members, and others in need in the community, with godly love and compassion. "This is my commandment, that ye love one another, as I have loved you. Greater love hath no man than this, that a man lay down his life for his friends." (John 15:12, 13(KJV))

Trust that the Lord will keep you from falling into sin and or getting caught up with those who lead ungodly lives. This means that we are to live holy before God trusting that He will keep us. "Now unto Him that is able to keep you from falling and to present you faultless before the presence of His glory with exceeding joy, To the only wise God our Savior, be glory and majesty, dominion and power, both now and ever, Amen." (Jude 24-25(KJV))

During our walk with the Lord we will experience hardships, i.e. victimization, persecution or ungodly acts, which come from the world but many times from other Believers for no apparent reason. This may be in the form of untrue accusations of any kind. To physically fight back the enemy with words using the tongue or any other physical means, can cause further trouble, as the enemy may not accuse you with an untruth to your face when they know they cannot verify an untruth. This is always a spiritual battle which cannot be fought by physical means. We are to hold on to the fact that God will vindicate his children, as a good Father would do. "Thou therefore endure hardness, as a good soldier of Jesus Christ. No man that warreth entangleth himself with the affairs of this life; that he may please Him who hath chosen him to be a Soldier (2Timothy 2:3-4(KJV)."

We are never to compromise our God-given freedom which we received with Salvation. The Apostle Paul soon learnt that it was better to stand for Christ in the early years of his salvation, while he faced so many trials. Thrown in prison over and over; Five separate times received 39 lashes from the Jews; In danger from his own people to name a few. Trials come to teach us to understand how to be stronger and patient while we press to walk by faith and waiting for vindication through Him. God has given us freedom to serve and love Him even as He continually strengthens us. "Stand fast therefore in the liberty wherewith Christ hath made us free and be not entangled with the yoke of bondage." (Galatians 5:1(KJV) Your encouragement shows up when you become discouraged in your trials, always be reminded of what Paul was confronted with during his Christian journey.

Whatever God grants us the power to do as we live in His Grace, believe it can be done. Regardless to whatever you go through, if you are a Believer God will make it possible to provide all you need, and at the same time, provide extra so that you can help others. Our duty is to just believe Him! "I can do all things through Christ which strengtheneth me. (Philippians 4:13(KJV)

Our sincere attitude towards the gospel which includes our treatment of others who are disadvantaged is seen by God, who rewards us by causing us to prosper and be in health as we keep His commandments. "Use hospitality one to another without grudging (1 Peter 4:9(KJV)."

Being honest is rarely easy for many Believers. But Jesus is totally honest and to tell lies would be moving away from him. Therefore, honesty within ourselves should be an important focus as we live for Him. "Jesus saith unto him, I am the way, the truth, and the life: no man cometh unto the Father, but by me (John 14:6(KJV)." Let's seek to be content to make honest, truthful decisions even if we will not be benefitted in the end. For instance, if someone else deserves the prize, i.e. to be highlighted, or performs better than yourself, step aside for that one without begrudging them.

God our Father and Jesus Christ, the Son (our brother), are one. So, when we believe the truth of the Word of God, we will become one. "That they all may be one; as thou, Father, art in me and I in thee, that they also may be one in us: that the world may believe that thou hast sent me." (John 17:21(KJV) Every Believer should pray to live in unity with other Believers.

Be resolved to Remain on the Right Course, thus fulfilling the Mandate which Jesus left us to complete.

Printed in the United States
by Baker & Taylor Publisher Services